Praise fo

THE **TEACHER'S POCKI**

EFFECTIVE CLASSROON

===

"Filled with powerful principles to promote
successful classrooms, this easy-to-read book
is a must read for all teachers."

===

—Linda M. Bambara, Ed.D.
Lehigh University

===

"Dr. Knoster hit the nail right on the head:
Relationships are everything, especially for
struggling learners. This book has been long
overdue. I hope that all future teachers will
have the opportunity to read it."

===

—Sharon Ann Ballard-Krishnan, RN
Parent of a student with autism

===

"Very user-friendly, with tons of great ideas
and strategies to use in the classroom to create a climate of acceptance and success for
all learners."

===

—Frances E. Clark, Ed.D.
Coordinator of Emotional/Behavior Disorders
West Virginia Department of Education
Office of Special Programs

"The perfect book to read at the start of each term to remind and refocus [educators]."

"Valuable and practical. . . . I thought of all my teacher friends and colleagues and how such a readable resource might improve their teaching lives and classrooms."

"An outstanding, easy-to-read guidebook that will be immensely useful for teachers, written by an author who knows what he is talking about. It is authoritative but written in an enjoyable, conversational style."

THE **TEACHER'S POCKET GUIDE** FOR

EFFECTIVE
CLASSROOM
MANAGEMENT

THE **TEACHER'S POCKET GUIDE** FOR

EFFECTIVE CLASSROOM MANAGEMENT

by

Tim Knoster, Ed.D.
School of Education
College of Professional Studies
Bloomsburg University of Pennsylvania

Baltimore • London • Sydney

Paul H. Brookes Publishing Co.
Post Office Box 10624
Baltimore, Maryland 21285-0624
USA

www.brookespublishing.com

Manufactured in the United States of America by
Versa Press, Inc., East Peoria, Illinois.

Library of Congress Cataloging-in-Publication Data
Knoster, Tim, 1956–
    The teacher's pocket guide for effective classroom management / by
    Tim Knoster.
       p.   cm.
    Includes bibliographical references.
    ISBN-13: 978-1-55766-918-6
    ISBN-10: 1-55766-918-X
    1. Classroom management.   2. Effective teaching.   I. Title.

    LB3013.K63 2008
    371.102'4—dc22   2008003950

British Library Cataloguing in Publication data are available from the
British Library.

2012   2011   2010   2009   2008

10   9   8   7   6   5   4   3   2   1

Contents

So Who Is This Guy?...................... vii

Acknowledgments ix

1   So Why Should I Read This Book?.......... 1

2   So Why Do Kids Act the Way
    They Do? 7

3   So How Do I Prevent Problem
    Behavior in My Classroom?............. 13
    Building Rapport
    Establishing Clear Expectations
    Reinforcing Expected Behavior

4   So How Close Should I Get with My
    Students? 23

5   So How Do I Go About Establishing
    Expectations in My Classroom? 33

6   So How Hard Is It to Use
    Reinforcement in My Classroom? 43

7   So Does It Really Boil Down to
    Classroom Climate? 59

8   So What Else Can I Do? 67

9   So How Do I Connect the Dots? 85

References and Resources
    for Further Reading.................... 91

Appendix................................ 95

So Who Is This Guy?

Tim Knoster, Ed.D., is an associate professor in the School of Education, College of Professional Studies, at Bloomsburg University of Pennsylvania and also serves as Executive Director of the international Association for Positive Behavior Support. Dr. Knoster (or Tim, as he prefers) has been involved with preservice and inservice teacher training since the mid-1980s. He has worn many hats throughout his career, including that  of classroom teacher, Director of Student Support Services and Special Education, and Principal Investigator on federal projects focused on classroom and student-centered behavior intervention and support. In addition, Dr. Knoster has extensive experience in providing professional development for classroom teachers throughout the United States and has been the recipient of various awards for his endeavors in this regard. He has extensively published manuscripts, training materials, and other practitioner-oriented resources concerning the linkages among research, policy, and practice in the classroom. Most important, Dr. Knoster has an uncanny ability to help teachers interpret the research literature on behavioral matters in a way that enables them to translate that same research into practical strategies and approaches in their classrooms. Along these same lines, Dr. Knoster has a national reputation of being a dynamic advocate, leader, and presenter concerning classroom management and student-centered behavior intervention and support.

Acknowledgments

Given that we are all influenced by so many people in our lives, it would require a better memory than I have, coupled with too many pages for the publisher to list specific names of all of the individuals who have influenced my work over the years. So...rather than try to create an exhaustive who's who list (as well as run the risk of inadvertently leaving someone out), I would like to acknowledge a few groups (or networks) of people in this regard.

First, I would like to thank my friends and colleagues involved with both the Association for Positive Behavior Support and the Positive Behavior Approaches Committee of TASH for the influence that they have had on my orientation to addressing behavioral concerns. The people within these networks know who they are and also operate from a similar perspective as mine in sharing the understanding that it is our collective work (rather than any one of us as individuals) that really matters.

In addition, I would like to acknowledge the professional challenges, encouragement, and support that I have received from my friends within the advocacy community in tandem with the countless numbers of teachers (and prospective teachers) with whom I have had the privilege to interact and collaborate over the years. Furthermore, it is these same people who have helped to keep me grounded in practical matters that mean the most to families and teachers and who continually remind me that while the work we do is important, I should not take myself too seriously.

Finally, and most important, I want to acknowledge as well as dedicate this book to my family and close friends who provide the color and flavor in my life. None of us is an island to him- or herself, and in this regard, it is these same people to whom I am indebted beyond my ability to repay. You provide meaning to my life along with the inspiration and support to share my thoughts (for better or worse).

So Why Should I Read This Book?

I believe there is one main reason why you should read this book (after ruling out personal reasons such as being a good friend or a relative of mine). You should find the content helpful if you work directly (or aspire to work directly) with young children or adolescents in a classroom setting. Let's face it—anyone who works with kids in schools knows first hand the rewards and challenges (the proverbial roller coaster ride of emotions with the highs and lows) that we can experience in our classrooms on a daily basis. Teachers have personal understanding of these shared experiences, whether it be big hugs or big tears from young children, high fives for a job well done, adolescent sneers over assigned work, or a poor grade on a project or test. If truth in advertising were provided to aspiring teachers, the statement, "Teaching can be hazardous to your health and is not recom-

mended for the faint of heart," would be visibly posted
on the walls at all teacher preparatory institutions.
The job of effectively teaching students becomes even
more daunting with the addition of increasing
demands for academic student performance as prima-
rily measured through high-stakes testing these days,
along with (what at least feels like at times) the pub-
licly posted bull's-eye or "kick me" sign that we as
teachers collectively wear on our backs in the eyes of
some factions within our society. It is with a firsthand
understanding of this societal context that I set out to
write this book, with the primary goal of providing my
fellow teachers with a helpful, user-friendly resource
to guide the establishment of a healthy classroom
environment for student learning. I believe you
will find this book, which in reality is
somewhat akin to a *Cliffs Notes* version
or connecting the dots of what I call
foundational classroom management
procedures, valuable regardless of
whether you are an aspiring high school
teacher or a veteran of more than 20
years in a kindergarten classroom. You should
also find these procedures useful regardless of
the age of your students as well as the presence or
absence of disability. Simply stated, I do not want to
waste your time in reading (or my time in writing) this
book for its own sake. After all, many traditional text-
books in the field outline and describe classroom management procedures. Why reinvent the wheel? As
such, this book is written in a conversational tone,
using first-person language, which I have used in
workshops and in-service training with thousands of
classroom teachers in various states. The practices
and approaches described are based in the literature

just like traditional texts on classroom management and therefore reflect evidence-based practice. I have chosen, however, to write in a conversational tone devoid of numerous citations embedded within the narrative for ease of reading and to enhance communication. A list of recommended resources is provided for you on pages 91–94 of this book if you desire to have access to the literature base that I have incorporated into these chapters. I am optimistic that you will find this book to be an easy read in terms of concepts and practice. Although each chapter can stand alone, I encourage you to look at the approaches highlighted in this book as a composite (or in total) because the practices described create what I propose to be

=============
Teaching can be hazardous to your health and is not recommended for the faint of heart.
=============

an overall picture (or Gestalt, so to speak) of effective classroom management. In other words, the whole is worth more than the sum of its parts, especially if those parts are viewed in isolation from one another. Furthermore, it is unlikely that you will find any one aspect of preventative practice highlighted to be, in and of itself, a panacea, silver bullet, or Holy Grail in terms of classroom management. Rather, the principles of practices described, when implemented in concert with one another, will help you to establish and/or maintain a healthy learning environment (i.e., classroom climate) that will in its own way help you to create a healthy balance between prevention and intervention as it pertains to student behavior in your classroom.

As has been noted by many, as teachers we not only touch the future, but we also help to create it as a result of our endeavors with our students. Our shared mission is to help our students learn and grow in a manner that enables each child to develop both academic and behavioral or social competence. Given that you are reading this now, it is very likely that you already have an appreciation for the fact that student growth and learning involves a lot of things. One way in which I think about growth and learning is based on my experiences in preservice and gradu-ate-level training of educators. In teacher preparation, teacher educators view growth and learning in students (current and future teachers) relevant to their acquisition of the necessary knowl-edge, skills, and dispositions to be effec-tive teachers. I believe that knowledge, skills, and dispositions are equally rele-vant for students from preschool through the 12th grade. In particular, I suggest that as teachers we are brokers of student growth in that we help our students to learn problem-solving skills that lend themselves to both academic/intellectual and social-emotional situa-tions. Helping our students become responsible citi-zens as adults is a tall order, and as teachers what we do and how we do it have a direct impact on how our students grow and learn. Along these same lines, I would argue that the center of the learning process in our schools today continues to be the classroom—each individual classroom—and the level of achievement directly related to the mentoring relationships that are established between the classroom teacher and his or her students. Establishing an effective learning com-munity within your classroom requires certain fea-tures to be present. The primary focus in Chapters 1–7 is to clearly 1) describe each of those preventative fea-tures, 2) help you to see the interconnectedness of these preventative features, and 3) provide you with

============

The center of the learning process in our schools today continues to be the classroom.

============

some guidance in approaches you can use to establish these preventative features holistically within your respective classroom setting. In addition, Chapter 8 provides a cursory overview of a continuum of reactive interventions to consider when responding to varying degrees of problem behavior, and Chapter 9 should help you connect all of the principles of practice described throughout Chapters 1–8. Furthermore, examples and illustrations of various aspects of classroom management procedures are provided in the Appendix for your convenience.

I appreciate the time you are taking to read this book. We can all relate to (at least on occasion) feeling like our time has been wasted on doing things that just don't seem to add up when it comes to making a difference with our students. I know first hand that there is nothing more frustrating than to feel like my time has been wasted on some task or activity that someone else has required me to do that just does not seem to be directly connected to my daily activities in the classroom. Time is an increasingly scarce commodity for all of us. As such, I thank you for your investment of time in reading this book and (most important) your time and energy in applying these principles of practice within your classroom.

So **Why Do Kids Act the Way They Do?**

So why do kids act the way that they do? Boy, if there was a short answer to that question I would share it with you (as well as the world) and make a couple million dollars in the process. I believe the key to understanding or decoding student behavior lies, first and foremost, in understanding our own actions and the nature of our own behavior. In other words, it is helpful to think about our own behavior and what influences how we act as a means to gaining a perspective about our students' behavior. I like to refer to this as thinking in the first person about our own personal experiences in order to understand others. In reality, there are causal roots behind why we act as we do within and across situations. As a general rule, our behavior, as well as our students' behavior, is not random (even though it may appear so from time to time). The interactive effect of both nature (or personal predispositions) and nurture (the things that happen to us or with us in our life circumstances) influences how each of us acts or reacts. For example, our reaction (action), whether we are experiencing extreme stress or feeling relaxed and calm, is similar to the parallel chain of events of our students, whether they are experiencing extreme stress or feeling relaxed and calm. If your life is anything like mine, then you have experienced a day in which things start out poorly when you leave for work and just seem to go downhill throughout the day in your classroom. Then, on returning home that same evening, you find that you are not as particularly nurturing toward others as you might be following a better day in the field. Sometimes those closest to you or around you are the first to notice your "altered state" and may, in fact, comment on it, which can have a similar effect as throwing gas onto smoldering embers. It can be combustible to say the least! It is not that you love those at home any less at that moment in time—to the contrary, what you may likely be looking for when stressed out is the unconditional love and support you have come to expect from those closest to you. When you are feeling exhausted and overwhelmed, however, the smallest thing tends to set you off, which can look ugly and make everyone involved feel unloved and underappreciated.

=============

The key to understanding or decoding student behavior lies, first and foremost, in understanding our own actions and the nature of our own behavior.

=============

Further compounding the confusing nature of decoding behavior is how some kids just seem to be more resilient and able to handle things better than other kids. For example, I am sure you have (at least) one kid that, regardless of what is thrown his or her way, is spontaneously reflexive and just always seems to land on his or her feet, much like a cat. Then there is _____ (you fill in the name here) who, despite all of your best wishes, intentions, and good faith efforts to structure activities to improve his or her success in the classroom, just always seems to have the uncanny ability to respond to situations as if there was a conspiracy that was out to get him or her. This type of experience with your students is similar to situations that you may face with your colleagues (i.e., some may be more resilient on a daily basis compared with others). It seems that some people (kids and adults) have more natural insulation against adverse elements in their respective worlds when compared with their peers.

So given all of this, is it simply people's nature to do better when under stress as compared with others? Or is it an issue of nurture in that we can engineer (alter) our situations and circumstances so that no one (student or colleague) is exposed to undue or unhealthy levels of stress? Nature (i.e., pathology) versus nurture (i.e., environment) is an age-old debate that has preoccupied many in the field and spawned some great movies such as *Trading Places*, starring Dan Aykroyd and Eddie Murphy. In reality, rarely are the important issues of life as clear cut as asking the question, "Is it X, or is it Y?" (even though complex issues have a tendency to be portrayed in simplistic soundbites in our society today). In other words, both nature and nurture affect how we (or our students or colleagues) act at any given moment in time, and how we act or react may change across situations or over time. Therefore, in the classroom it looks as clear as mud on some given days, and this convoluted mess we call life can become even harder to understand when we allow ourselves to get trapped into

============

Rarely are the important issues of life as clear cut as asking the question, "Is it X, or is it Y?"

============

playing the unproductive either–or game of nature versus nurture.

So how do you go about making sense of all of this? I mean, practically, what is a teacher supposed to do with all of this in the classroom? Well, the key is in understanding that 1) all behavior (even challenging behavior) helps the person engaging in the behavior to address unmet needs as seen from his or her perspective in that behavior serves a purpose (technically referred to as a function) coupled with 2) realizing that behavior is context-related or situational. As such, the key to understanding why your kids act as they do and, in turn, helping these same kids to grow and learn in your classroom, is to acknowledge the existence of what you cannot control (e.g., nature, pathology) while at the same time investing your time and energy on the things you can influence (e.g., your classroom environment). The reality is that parents send the best kids that they have to school; they do not keep the better ones at home. You inherit, so to speak, the kids in your classroom at any given moment in time. As such, your job then becomes working with those kids in a manner that helps you to meet them where they are at in order to help them grow and learn over time. Understanding the nature of behavior and the importance of context can help you more efficiently understand why your students act as they do. In real estate, selling a home is (mostly) about location, location, location, and understanding student behavior is (mostly) about context, context, context. As a teacher, you have a direct influence on the context for learning within your classroom.

> ==============
> The reality is that parents send the best kids that they have to school; they do not keep the better ones at home.
> ==============

Although each student you have within your classroom may respond differently at different times, and some may be, in fact, more resilient than others due to their natural genetic predisposition coupled with their life experiences prior to coming into your classroom, it is your work (the professional work of a teacher) to engineer your classroom so that all of your students experience academic and behavioral success. Or, to quote Ginott:

> I have come to a frightening conclusion. I am the decisive element in the classroom. It is my personal approach that creates the climate. It is my daily mood that makes the weather. As a teacher, I possess tremendous power to make a child's life miserable or joyous. I can be a tool of torture or an instrument of inspiration. I can humiliate or humor, hurt or heal. In all situations it is my response that decides whether a crisis will be escalated or de-escalated, and a child humanized or de-humanized. (1972, pp. 15–16)

So How Do I Prevent Problem Behavior in My Classroom?

Your perspective, whether limited to your classroom or more broadly in life, directly affects how you interpret the events in your daily life. Developing perspective is a funny thing because it is a highly personalized experience and, much like art, interpreted in the eye of the beholder. Mark Twain has been credited with saying, "It ain't what you don't know that will get you in trouble, it's what you know for sure that just ain't so." Simply stated, a terminal degree of certainty is a dangerous thing to have about anything, most specifically about human behavior. The reality is that you will be unable to prevent all inappropriate behavior from ever occurring within your classroom—unless each of your students is either Mother Teresa incarnate or your classroom has no students. Rather, what you can do is establish a few basic operating procedures that will enhance the learning environment in a way that can

============
The primary emphasis in effective classroom management is preventing student problem behavior in the first place.
============

============
Realistically, you will
never be able to
control all student
behavior.
============

dramatically reduce the likelihood of both nuisance and problem behaviors.

Nuisance behaviors are those that in and of themselves are essentially inconsequential, such as the student who appears fidgety and calls out to get your attention as opposed to raising his or her hand. It is often inconsequential behavior that should be ignored, however, that historically (or perhaps hysterically) has been known to get strong adverse reactions from teachers.

Yet, problem behavior must be immediately stopped, and the student must be redirected to act in a more appropriate manner. For example, a student who is taking materials from another student must be told by the teacher, "Stop taking John's book and answer sheet. I want you to open your own book and do your work on your own." Perspective—*your* perspective to be specific—comes into play in understanding that inappropriate behaviors are not always equal and, realistically, you will never be able to control all student behavior. This may seem like an odd statement to make from someone providing guidance on classroom management, but it is an important concept to understand because it can dramatically affect your perspective and subsequent approach to classroom management.

One of my personal pet peeves with regard to behavior management comes from the term *management*, which has become commonplace in the field. The very term implies this false notion of control in that it suggests that you will manage your students as if they were collectively nothing more than raw material to be organized within your classroom. I don't know about you, but I know I have enough difficulty managing my own behavior (especially on tough days), let alone managing anyone else's behavior. Now, having said this, there are things that you can manage that will help you have a direct positive effect on your students' behavior. The nature of these things that you can control (or at least greatly influence) ironically has less to do with your students' behavior and more to do with how you act or do not act on a daily basis in your classroom. I think a more accurate descriptor for group and classroom management is "Teacher Self-Management of Instructional Practice in Group Settings," but this title is far too long and will understandably not be accepted in the field. So I will use the term *classroom management* for simplicity's sake. Having said this, the important thing to keep in mind is not so much the term but the idea I am trying to communicate.

Developing a classroom management plan can appear daunting from the onset. I mean, there are just so many things to take into account and plan for, and then you have to think about individualizing for unique student needs. Although there are various aspects to consider when designing a game plan for your classroom, it helps to keep things simple. For example, classroom management can be viewed as having two main themes: prevention and intervention. Understandably, it is easy to become preoccupied with finding the answer(s) to the question, "What do I do when a student does X?" Although you will need a set of standard operating procedures to efficiently

and safely redirect student problem behavior, the primary emphasis in effective classroom management is preventing problem behavior in the first place. A simple way to think about this is as follows: If you consider all of the time that you will invest in managing student behavior in your classroom, then a minimum of 80% of that behavior management time should be invested in preventative approaches. This so-called 80–20 split (80% prevention, 20% intervention) is generally accepted within the professional literature and is borne out daily within effective classrooms. Having noted this proportional weighting of your invested time in behavior management, there are precise tactics of teaching, or principles of practice, that are relevant to both prevention as well as intervention of student problem behavior. In particular, three specific principles of practice in prevention serve as the foundation for effective classroom management that are within your immediate control as a classroom teacher. Regardless of the type of classroom you operate (e.g., elementary, secondary general, or special education), the following principles of practice are relevant for you.

> ============
> The primary emphasis in effective classroom management is preventing problem behavior in the first place.
> ============

1. Rapport

2. Clear expectations

3. Reinforcement of expected behavior

These three approaches, when viewed in total and in concert with one another, may best be visualized as a three-legged stool of prevention in which each component is somewhat interdependent on the presence of the other two components in order to bear the weight of student behavior in your classroom.

The importance of establishing rapport with your students is (for the most part) a universally accepted understanding in our schools today. Oddly enough, however, many teachers struggle on a daily basis with establishing rapport with all of their students, especially those who appear difficult to reach. In other words, we kind of have an understanding as teachers as to why connecting with our students is important, but as a field, we are somewhat limited in our understanding of time-efficient, systematic practices that we can use to establish rapport. Thinking of your own personal experiences in your classroom, you most likely have established rapport with those students with whom you are most comfortable. More often than not, these are the kids who provide you with a lot of reinforcement and are least likely to develop problem behavior over time. As such, you likely would describe these kids as your favorites. To be clear, and for the record, you are a person first and a professional second. Therefore, you will have favorites, and acknowledging this reality is an important first step to establishing rapport with your students who are more difficult to reach. In our personal lives, we get to choose those with whom we hang out. As teachers, however, we don't have the luxury or right to pick and choose whom we will successfully work with within our classrooms.

You will likely find yourself naturally gravitating toward your favorite students, as this is human nature (hey, we all would rather hang out with others who make us feel good). The professional challenge is to

> ============
> You will have favorites, and acknowledging this reality is an important first step to establishing rapport with your students who are more difficult to reach.
> ============

1) understand this aspect of human nature and 2) reach out and connect with those students who appear more distant from you in terms of personal comfort. Therefore, it is important to have a few time-efficient methods in your teacher "bag of tricks" that can help you establish a conducive level of rapport with each of your students—not just the ones toward whom you naturally gravitate. When it comes to effective teaching and rapport, the bottom line is that most kids don't care what you know as a teacher until they know that you really care about them as people (Albert, 1996). As such, it is helpful to put into practice some simple rapport-building techniques on a regular basis that will help each of your students increasingly understand that you really do care about them on a personal level. If you are anything like most teachers that I know, you are a nurturing, fun-loving, and approachable person, but for a number of reasons, not all of your students will see you in this light (at least not right away, and especially not those students who may appear to be most at risk to develop problem behavior). I will describe these rapport-building strategies in greater detail in Chapter 4 as they should prove helpful to you in reaching out and sufficiently connecting with all of the kids in your classroom.

Establishing a classroom environment conducive to learning (and developing rapport with each of your students) is enhanced by establishing a clear set of behavioral expectations. In

============
If you are anything like most teachers that I know, you are a nurturing, fun-loving, and approachable person, but for a number of reasons, not all of your students will see you in this light.
============

other words, rapport becomes a byprod-
uct of your endeavors within the classroom, and although some teaching
strategies can help you to establish rapport, the effect of these tactics is greatly
enhanced when used in tandem with
clear social-performance expectations.
Establishing expectations is all about
developing a set of cultural norms within
your classroom and ultimately about fos-
tering social competence in all of your

============
You want to be
sure that you are
sailing in a direction
that has some
promising land
ahead, instead
of large icebergs
to strike.
============

students. To be clear, I am not talking about simply
creating a list of rules or a list of "thou shalt nots."
Rather, what I am referring to is identifying between
three to five broad expectations toward which you will
foster growth and progress with each of your students
on an ongoing basis (e.g., be respectful, be responsible, be safe). Now, I am sure you may be thinking,
"This is too simple. I mean, it can't be that simple, can
it?" Well, although there is more operational detail
regarding expectations that you will need to address,
starting at such a basic level steers you in the right
direction. As the Greek philosopher Seneca noted, "If
one does not know to which port one is sailing, no wind is favorable." Simply stated,
you want to be sure that you are sailing
in a direction that has some promising
land ahead, instead of large icebergs to
strike. Focusing your students' attention
toward what you want them to do (instead
of what you don't want them to do) is one of the
most important first steps you can take.

Your second step is to focus attention on more
operationally defining these three to five expectations
across important settings (and routines) throughout

your given classroom day, thus creating not only a road map for behavior for your students but also a radar system for you to use in terms of reinforcing your students as they demonstrate appropriate behavior per your expectations. Establishing three to five broadly stated expectations (and subsequently defining these expectations across settings and routines with your students) also creates a healthy degree of predictability that helps your students realize that they can influence or have some degree of power over their own personal degree of success in your classroom (also known as locus of control). Steps and procedures to use to engage your students in the process of establishing behavioral expectations for your classroom are provided in Chapter 5.

Reinforcement is the third principle of practice in this three-legged stool of preventative approaches to classroom management. Look, we all know that we can attract more bees with honey or more ants with sugar. What I mean to say is, the best way to help students develop appropriate behavior is by being clear on expected behavior and, as the saying goes, "catching them being good." I know, I know, this is not a novel concept, but I never said I was going to share new earth-shattering ideas with you. What I did say—even promise you—was that I would help you to develop a new perspective about classroom management that enables you to bring together (in full force) the basic aspects of prevention that will help you to increasingly become a more effective educator. Simply stated, reinforcement serves as one of the three cornerstones of prevention (well, if you can have cornerstones associated with a three-legged stool).

Aristotle has been attributed with saying, "We are what we repeatedly do, therefore excellence is not an act—but a habit." Let me expand a bit on this notion: Each of us is going to form habits, and our habits, good or bad, develop over time in association with what we are reinforced for doing. Whether it is the habit of kindness or of thievery, the principle of reinforcement (along with other factors) is in play. Instructionally, the goal becomes to help your students develop behavioral habits that are consistent with the social competencies you wish to see in your classroom. Reinforcing your students for performing expected behavior should increasingly become the norm in your classroom. In addition, it is important to understand that there are various forms of reinforcement and that not all reinforcement procedures—and most certainly not all reinforcers used by you as a teacher—will be equal. As such, it is important to understand the nature of positive and negative reinforcement and to further appreciate that what is actually reinforcing is (much like interpreting a work of art) in the eyes of the beholder (or the one being reinforced). Make no mistake about it, both positive and negative reinforcement are just that: forms of reinforcement to increase the likelihood of future recurrence of desired behavior. Positive reinforcement, however, is the name of the game as you will see in greater detail in Chapter 6.

Rapport, expectations, and reinforcement serve as three principles of practice in prevention of student problem behavior in your classroom. Each principle of practice is important in its own right; however, the sum is worth far more than the total of its parts. As

> Reinforcing your students for performing expected behavior should increasingly become the norm in your classroom.

such, let's turn our attention to each of these principles of practice and, in turn, focus on specific teaching strategies along these same lines.

So How Close Should I Get with My Students?

On understanding students as people

I recall one particular teacher that I had in high school who was simply brilliant in terms of his knowledge of the English language, breadth of understanding of American and European literature, and his ability to write in a manner that was succinct yet full of depth and description. Mr. Brice was incredibly gifted in the subject matter for which he had an understandable passion. Most (if not all) of his students (including yours truly), however, learned very quickly that Mr. Brice's passion clearly started and ended there. His approach to teaching could be summed up by saying he taught English to students rather than teaching students English. I, by no stretch of the imagination, would never be accused of being gifted when it comes to the English language. I couldn't tell you the difference between a dangling participle and a hanging curve ball other than I know from first-hand experience that if you are not careful, a hanging

23

===============
Mr. Brice's approach
to teaching could
be summed up by
saying he taught
English to students
rather than teaching
students English.
===============

curve ball can knock your lights out. Despite my lack of expertise with the English language, I was a relatively decent student in high school and (for the most part) tried my best to succeed. I really struggled with Mr. Brice's class, however. At the time, I chalked it up to my shortcomings as a student, despite the fact that it seemed that everyone I knew also struggled with Mr. Brice, even the students in our honors program. In retrospect, what I have come to appreciate is that regardless of all the natural talent Mr. Brice had in the English language, he clearly struggled with student language because he did not communicate (or did not care to communicate) any interest in us as people first—let alone as students enrolled in his class.

I also recall vividly another teacher from my high school days, Mr. Boyer for American history and world cultures. Mr. Boyer was a real hoot because he was always hanging around with his students (including myself), joking around, asking how we were doing, and going out of his way to help, even when it meant some extra work on his end. He clearly was a competent teacher in terms of both his knowledge of the subject matter and his understanding of students. What is amazing to me to this day is that I still have so many vivid memories of not only course content but also the things that we did during class time. Suffice it to say, Mr. Boyer's approach to teaching was that he taught students the value

===============
Mr. Boyer's
approach to
teaching was that
he taught students
the value of history
as opposed to try-
ing to force the
teaching of history
on his students.
===============

of history as opposed to trying to force the teaching of history on his students.

I have shared this bit of my personal experience as a student to set the stage for helping you to understand the importance of establishing rapport. Along these same lines, my goal in sharing this story is to help you develop some insight into approaches that can work for you in your endeavors to teach your students the value of the curriculum as opposed to simply teaching the curriculum to your students. We all live our lives in the first person (seeing things through personal eyes rather than professional eyes), and as such, a personal approach that is student centered (as opposed to subject centered) is in many ways a necessary first step in creating an effective learning environment in your classroom where all of your kids can thrive. The short of it is as follows: Regardless of prerequisite knowledge and/or interest in any given subject on the part of your students, your students will become increasingly motivated to learn and perform in your classroom if they understand that you have a genuine interest in them as people.

Creating a suitable level of rapport with your students will be, in many ways, an absolute essential prerequisite for their achievement, especially those that appear the most difficult to reach. Establishing rapport does not mean that you have to become each of your students' best friend. Rather, it means gaining a closeness with each of your stu-

==============
Your students will become increasingly motivated to learn and perform in your classroom if they understand that you have a genuine interest in them as people.
==============

dents in a way that positions you in each student's eyes as having his or her best interest at heart, even when the things you may be asking the student to do at a particular point in time are not high on his or her priority list. Such trusting relationships, which in turn help with student motivation, require thoughtful planting and tilling of the soil (like a garden). Classroom soil, so to speak, that is conducive to student learning does not simply produce growth on its own. Rather, growth is supported through your approach to teaching.

So where do you start? How do you put in place the procedures that help you to get and stay connected with your students? Well, with many of your students, the process will be quite easy; however, with a few, it will require a systematic approach. What typically happens for most teachers is that you will—in a natural manner that will not be particularly conscious on your part—begin to develop rapport and a suitably close relationship with some of your kids sooner than others. Over the course of time, you will increasingly become closer with this subset of your students to the degree that an outside observer to your classroom might describe this group of students as your "favorites." As I said in Chapter 3, it is both natural and predictable that you will have favorites (which is not necessarily the same as showing favoritism). The good news is that you will not need to spend much (if any) time thinking about establishing rapport with these students because the relationships will develop naturally. Your students who are harder to reach will be the ones with whom you need to employ a systematic process to establish rapport. In other words, these are the kids that do not, by their mere presence, provide you personally with a lot of positive reinforcement. And yes, it is these kids in particular that you are paid as a professional to teach. This last statement may appear a bit blunt or harsh, but I do believe it to be true. Just as you will naturally develop favorites, you will also be prone to develop least favorites in relation to those kids that you increasingly view as at risk for developing prob-

==============
Your students who are harder to reach will be the ones with whom you need to employ a systematic process to establish rapport.
==============

lem behavior. In other words, the types of feelings that your students who are harder to reach conjure in you will likely require you to act in a professional manner and to defy your basic human nature to increasingly avoid interactions with others who do not provide you with a lot of positive reinforcement. (I mean who wants to—out of choice—be around others who don't make you feel good.) You should thoughtfully and consistently increase your use of procedures that help you to connect in order to nurture rapport with your students who are at risk for developing behavioral problems.

There are two primary aspects to building rapport. First, we need to look at the precise steps or actions involved with getting close to your students. Second, we need to look at the application of these steps and procedures in the context of suitable situations within which to use these rapport-building procedures.

Rapport building, as with any other form of teaching activity, can be broken down into a series of steps through task analysis. The component steps represent links within an entire chain of events. In this sense, the following sequence of steps is involved when systematically building rapport with your students (see Table 4.1).

The steps associated with rapport building may also be viewed as component parts of basic interpersonal communication skills (in their simplest sense). As such, this task analysis may also be used when providing direct instruction to particular students who require it in order to learn basic social interaction skills.

At first glance, understanding the mechanics of building rapport appears relatively easy. Nervousness and anxiety complicate applying these steps because it is risky to reach out in this manner to a student (or

Table 4.1. Steps in building rapport

Demonstrate close proximity (move toward the student and be within arms reach).

Demonstrate age-appropriate touch (e.g., shake hands, high five).

Demonstrate appropriate facial expressions (reflect the nature of the situation).

Demonstrate appropriate tone of voice (voice matches situation).

Demonstrate appropriate body language (e.g., appear relaxed, keep arms open, be attentive, look at student).

Ask open-ended positive questions (e.g., "What are you doing after school?" "How do you do so well in your track meets?" "What was your favorite part of the movie?"). If you ask questions that require one-word answers, then that is what you will likely get from a student with whom you are not already close.

Listen while the student is speaking. Ideally, talk less than the student (try not to interrupt or abruptly change the topic).

Demonstrate the use of empathy statements. Act like a mirror and reflect the child's feelings by expressing your understanding and caring.

Ignore nuisance behavior and let the little stuff slide (but not problem behavior if it surfaces).

Stay cool throughout the process, which can be easier said than done.

Source: Latham, 1999.

small number of students) with whom you are already feeling distant. Having a clear understanding of these steps, as simple as they may appear, can be reassuring to you when you begin to make your proverbial leap of faith toward a few particular students. Beyond the basic mechanics of building rapport, it is also important to spend some time talking about appropriate situations in which to employ these procedures.

To explain the process of reaching out, think about some experiences in your own personal life. Specifically, think back to some point in time when you were at some social gathering (e.g., holiday party, hanging out with friends). Let's say you are at this event where you know some, but not all, of the guests. Suddenly, you see this person whom you do not know but would really like to get to know (call it physical attraction if you want). Now, if you are like most people that I know, even though you may think you're courageous, you would not just take the risk and "go for it" by approaching this person. In reality, you probably gave some time and thought to a number of things. Specifically, you were likely thinking about 1) how to approach him or her, 2) someone that you know who already knows him or her, 3) what types of things are of interest to him or her, and 4) a natural way (so it does not seem contrived) to bump into him or her to have a conversation, and so forth. In other words, you likely gave many things a lot of thought (even if it was within a very short period of time). You were concerned about these things for a number of reasons, which can generally be summarized as "you never get a second chance to make a first impression."

Now, with this as a mental context, think about that particular kid with whom you need to get closer. You will want to give serious thought to his or her interests (e.g., music, sports, art). Furthermore, you will need to think about appropriate situations in which you can constructively get some level of dialogue started with him or her regarding these interests. What I am talking about here is what I like to describe as "ice breakers." The key is that you need some way to engage the student in a conversation about his or her interests within a safe/targeted situation in order to start the process of building rapport.

=============
You never get a
second chance
to make a first
impression.
=============

Now, to do this, you will likely have to give some time and thought (conduct some research, so to speak) to figure out what interests to tap into as well as what situations to target. You are looking for opportunities within the student's typical daily routine that are noninstructional times that would lend themselves to social interaction (e.g., during homeroom or lunch, transitions between classes, or after-school events) so that your interactions are not dependent on the student being successful with any given task. You want to provide free access to your attention (noncontingent) in this sense.

Along these same lines, it is important to understand that you can use rapport-building procedures in a couple of ways, either in a one-to-one situation with the focus student or in small-group situations using other students, with whom your rapport is stable, as social brokers with the student of concern. There is no one right way that is necessarily better than the other to start the process. My best advice is to pick one that you feel the most comfortable with or one that you are the least uncomfortable with as you plan your approach. Ideally, you will find yourself using a combination of these approaches as your confidence grows with your students.

On building rapport

For example, Jimmy is a student with whom you are feeling increasingly distant. You have done some investigative work and found out that he is really into video gaming. It just so happens that he is a part of the video gaming club at your middle school. As such, you begin to look for opportunities (short snippets of time) during club time at school as well as during the common lunch period that you share with Jimmy to ask his advice on videogame purchases for a friend's kid. You continue to explore ways to have brief conversations with Jimmy over the course of a couple weeks to the point at which after a month or so Jimmy occasionally goes out of his way to find you to ask if your friend bought the games and if his son liked them.

The final point on applying rapport-building strategies is to understand that a given student with whom you feel distant will unlikely open up for you after your first attempt to break the ice. Sometimes it will happen, but this is more the exception to the rule. It is more likely that incrementally, over time, a given student will gradually allow you to get closer to him or her as his or her comfort level with you grows. In other words, like most aspects of complex relationships, it will take time to evolve. The key in using rapport-building procedures is to use them whenever and wherever you find (or can create) the opportunity. Although you will not be able to predict how long it will take with any given student, the one thing you can have confidence in is that the relationship will likely improve over the course of time. Also, understand that unlike the personal social interaction that I asked you to reflect on earlier, your intent with any particular student with any given rapport-building encounter is not for a long-term interaction at that moment in time. Rather, rapport-building procedures applied in this fashion usually take as little time as between 30 seconds and 2 minutes depending on the situation. Therefore, the key (or power) is in the cumulative effect over time based on your repeated interactions with your students.

============

Over time, a given student will gradually allow you to get closer to him or her as his or her comfort level with you grows.

============

Now, as important as rapport-building procedures are—and make no mistake about it, they are important—they represent only one of the proverbial legs on the three-legged stool of prevention. In other words, establishing a good working rapport with all of your students will get you so far, but by itself it will be insufficient in terms of classroom management. It is important to combine such strategies to connect with your students by establishing clear and reasonably high behavioral expectations for everyone to follow within the classroom. As such, let's turn our attention to establishing expectations with your students—the second leg in our three-legged stool of effective classroom management.

So **How Do I Go About Establishing Expectations in My Classroom?**

It is helpful to be familiar with the past as we forge toward the future. As such, I thought you might enjoy a quick glimpse in the rearview mirror into the past of school discipline, and in particular, codes of conduct from the early 1900s (see Table 5.1). I find the behavioral concerns (and corresponding consequences) from this era whimsically of interest. In particular, if "boys and girls playing together" is worth four lashes, then it really makes me wonder

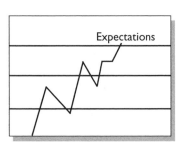

what they had in mind in terms of "misbehaving girls" (10 lashes). I mean, my imagination is really running wild on this one. What if those girls were playing cards while misbehaving around the creek, mill, or barn? Anyway, beyond the humor in looking into the past, there is one important aspect to grasp relevant to our disciplinary history. The behaviors noted (although reflective of that particular era) emphasize an exclusively punitive approach to estab-

Table 5.1. School discipline circa 1900

Offense	Punishment
Boys and girls playing together	4 lashes
Fighting at school	5 lashes
Quarreling at school	5 lashes
Gambling and betting at school	4 lashes
Playing cards at school	10 lashes
Climbing each foot over 3 feet up a tree	1 lash
Telling lies	7 lashes
Telling tales out of school	8 lashes
Giving each other ill names	3 lashes
Swearing at school	8 lashes
Misbehaving girls	10 lashes
Drinking spirituous liquor at school	8 lashes
Wearing long fingernails	2 lashes
Misbehaving to people on the road	4 lashes
Boys going to girls' play places	3 lashes
Girls going to boys' play places	3 lashes
Coming to school with dirty face and hands	2 lashes
Calling each other liars	4 lashes
Wetting each other washing at playtime	2 lashes
Scuffling at school	4 lashes
Going or playing about the creek	6 lashes
Doing mischief about the barn or mill	7 lashes

Sources: Gatto, n.d.; ThinkQuest, n.d.

lishing behavioral expectations. In other words, what is provided is simply a list of proverbial "thou shalt nots," with varying degrees of retribution for various offenses. Although one should always look at the nature of the times in question whenever considering historical aspects of schools and society, it is interesting that many classroom management approaches in some schools today could also be described as a modern day list of "thou shalt nots." In other words, although we could change items such as "scuffling at school" to "no bullying," the emphasis of such approaches is on what *not* to do rather than on a more constructive approach. Both the literature and experience tell us that the most effective way to influence student behavior is by being clear about what you want your students to do and reinforcing your students when they do it. Although it is certainly relevant to have naturally occurring consequences for student misbehavior (short of the "lashes," of course), such consequences are most effective when delivered in concert with high levels of positive reinforcement for expected behavior. For example, it is certainly understandable that you (and I) do not want to see students bullying other students in our classrooms. Having said this, however, the most effective way to minimize the likelihood of such problem behavior is by investing our time and attention on reinforcing alternative appropriate behaviors (e.g., being respectful toward others). On the surface, this may seem like nothing more than a game of semantics, but when you look at this in the larger scheme of classroom management, it is as different as sailing east compared with sailing west. For the record, I am neither naive nor am I proposing that you take what might be understandably dismissed as a Walden Two approach to classroom management (where life is beautiful all the time and we sit around giving group hugs and singing "Kumbaya"). Look, we all need to have specific procedures and consequences in place in our classrooms for problem behavior. The key to preventing problem behavior from occurring in

============

Although it is certainly relevant to have naturally occurring consequences for student misbehavior…, such consequences are most effective when delivered in concert with high levels of positive reinforcement for expected behavior.

============

Table 5.2. Fundamental aspects of establishing clear behavioral expectations in the classroom

Select three to five positively stated, broad behavioral expectations.

Identify your highest priority settings and/or routines within which you anticipate the greatest likelihood of student problem behavior.

Operationally define each of your three to five expectations across each of your identified settings/routines by asking yourself, "What would my students look and sound like if they were being successful?" Try to engage your students in the process.

Post your behavioral expectations prominently in your classroom.

Provide initial instruction concerning your expectations at the start of the year, and provide booster sessions periodically throughout the school year.

Reinforce your students on a regular basis for appropriate behavior—catch them being good.

Have clear, systematic (and reasonable) consequences for student problem behavior.

the first place, however, is establishing clear expectations for desired behavior and reinforcing our students as they perform those same behaviors on a regular basis.

Establishing student behavioral expectations in the classroom (and schools in general) has received much attention over the years. Most recently, however, there has been increased discussion in the field about implementing expectations that make sense and are feasible for any classroom teacher. In other words, breathing life into what the research literature suggests works in a manner that is both useful and user friendly. Table 5.2 reflects the fundamental aspects of establishing expectations so that the students in your classroom increasingly demonstrate social competence, which helps you to set the stage for developing academic competence with each of your students as a result of increased achievement in your classroom.

As the old saying goes, one needs to know the bull's eye if one is to be held accountable for hitting the mark. As such, you need to start by identifying three to five (no more, no less) broad behavioral expectations that encompass the types of social behaviors you desire in your students (e.g., be responsible, be respectful, be ready). There is not an exclusive set of

============

Breathing life into what the research literature suggests works in a manner that is both useful and user friendly.

============

expectations in the literature for use in your classroom; the key is to identify expectations that make sense to you in your specific classroom. Have fun with acronyms and mnemonics as you see appropriate. For example, some teachers have used the "Three Bees" noted previously and subsequently have employed a bumble bee motif throughout the year in their classroom. Other teachers have successfully used different sets of expectations to create phrases such as STARS (*S*trive to succeed, *T*ry your best, *A*chieve to your potential, *R*espect yourself and others, and *S*afety first) or SOAR (*S*afe, *O*rganized, *A*ttentive, and *R*esponsible).

Identifying your broad expectations is the first step in establishing student behavioral expectations in your classroom. The next step is to think about your classroom and the types of activities you will have the students do within your classroom. As you think about your classroom, think about both settings and routines within your classroom that have historically produced the greatest likelihood of student behavioral errors. If you are new to your classroom this year, then think about the types of situations that might predictably

	Setting/ Routine 1	Setting/ Routine 2	Setting/ Routine 3	Setting/ Routine 4	Setting/ Routine 5	Setting/ Routine 6
Expectation 1						
Expectation 2						
Expectation 3						
Expectation 4						
Expectation 5						

Figure 5.1. Planning matrix for establishing behavioral expectations.

have the greatest likelihood to create either confusion or problem behavior with your students. In other words, what situations/contexts are most likely to give you the biggest headaches in terms of classroom management. Specifically, think about physical locations within your room (e.g., coat area, supply areas, workstations/lab areas) in combination with high frequency routines associated with your expectations (e.g., getting to work right away on independent work, asking for help when needed, sharing materials and supplies during group tasks). Identifying five or six of your highest priority settings and routines is a necessary next step to breathe operational life into your expectations. I encourage you to use the matrix depicted in Figure 5.1 for planning purposes once you have identified your expectations as well as your priority settings/routines within your classroom.

You are now ready to take the final step in establishing your behavioral expectations once you have plugged your broad expectations into the left-hand side of this planning matrix and your priority settings/ routines across the top. The next step is to operationally define each of your expectations across each of your priority settings/ routines. The most important reason for this is that appropriate behavior will likely look different from setting to setting or routine to routine (e.g., being responsible while doing independent seat work looks and sounds different than being responsible while doing group work). A simple way to think about operationally defining any given expectation is to simply ask yourself, "What would my students look and sound like if they were meeting this expectation within this setting/routine?" Furthermore, along these same lines, asking this question significantly increases the likelihood of operationally defining expected behaviors that are desirable as opposed to creating a modern day version of "thou shalt nots." To help you in this regard, I encourage you to apply the "dead man test" to any behavioral expectation that you establish in your classroom. Once you have defined an expectation within each setting/routine, ask yourself, "Could a dead person perform this expectation as stated?" If you answer "yes" (e.g., a dead person excels at "no pushing or shoving others"), then go back to the drawing board because your behavioral expectation is in need of repair. Applying the "dead man test" can help you minimize the likelihood of defining your broad expectations in terms of statements such as "no running, no stealing, no fighting, no swearing," all the way

> ============
> A simple way to think about operationally defining any given expectation is to simply ask yourself, "What would my students look and sound like if they were meeting this expectation within this setting/routine?"
> ============

===========

If a dead person
can perform the
expectation, then
it is probably not a
particularly useful
behavioral expecta-
tion in terms of
reinforcement.

===========

up through "no boys going into girl play spaces." In other words, if a dead person can perform the expectation, then it is probably not a particularly useful behavioral expectation in terms of reinforcement. Applying the "dead man test" in this manner can also help you reduce the likelihood of awkward moments with that one kid who always seems to be able to find the gray space between lists of rules when presented in the form of "thou shalt nots" by saying, "That wasn't on the list of things we couldn't do." I know... I know... each of us always seems to have one particular kiddo like this in the classroom who can drive you crazy to the point of really needing to fight the urge on a particularly difficult day of saying something to the effect of, "Well, public flogging is not on the list either, shall I just go ahead and chain you all to the whipping post now?" But of course the cooler, more professional side of your brain kicks in to help you refrain from making such a statement (at least out loud). Anyway, I think you get my point in this regard. The Appendix at the end of this book includes examples of behavioral expectation matrices from various elementary, middle, and high school classrooms to help get you started.

We all generally accept the notion that good instructonal practice engages students actively as learners in our classrooms. As such, actively engaging your students in the process of defining your expectations across setting/routines is highly encouraged. Although there are a number of good reasons to consciously consider doing this, the biggest reasons are that by doing so you 1) are actually preteaching the expectations as a result of the process of asking the kids to help you define the expectations and 2) increase the degree and rate of "buy-in" (motivation) as you are providing increasing degrees of locus of control for each of your students by having them help you define the expectations within the parameters you have provided. This, much like the initial selection of your broad expectations, can take on many forms. The key is to find the way with which you are most comfortable in engaging your students in the process. For example, at the beginning of the school year, have each student come up with some privately developed operational definitions and then have your kids do some pair-share work leading up to large-group discussion in your classroom. Another way is to simply engage your students in structured large-group discussion on the first day of school and (depending on the age and nature of your students) have them develop skits and/or demonstrations comparing and contrasting the appropriate versus inappropriate ways in which to act. Your professional judgment, of course, will serve as your primary navigational device along these same lines. The key is that you can engage your students in the process and actually have fun based on what you believe is the best way to go in your classroom.

    As with any aspect of effective teaching, it is important to provide clear expectations for performance coupled with reinforcement for performance of your expectations on an ongoing basis. It is important to post your established behavioral expectations to support your students to collectively act in a

> It is important to post your established behavioral expectations to support your students to collectively act in a manner that creates a culture of social competence within your classroom.

manner that creates a culture of social competence within your classroom. This will occur over time as not only as students are reminded by the public posting and your reinforcement procedures but also particularly as students begin to prompt appropriate social behavior from one another on a regular basis. Public posting will also serve as a visual reminder for you to "catch your kids being good" for the purpose of reinforcement, which leads us to the third leg of the proverbial three-legged stool of effective classroom management: reinforcement procedures.

So How Hard Is It to Use Reinforcement in My Classroom?

So what is reinforcement, and, in particular, how should reinforcers be used in the classroom? There are two types of reinforcement: positive and negative. Understanding the similarities and differences between these two forms of reinforcement will set the stage for a conversation about selecting and using reinforcers with students in your classroom as a part of your management system.

By definition (and yes, it will be necessary to use some jargon for a bit so please bear with me), *positive reinforcement* is the presentation of a desired stimulus contingent on the performance of a desired behavior in order to increase the likelihood of future recurrence of that same desired behavior (e.g., verbally praising a student [presuming that he or she finds verbal praise desirable] after he or she demonstrated an expected social skill [e.g.,

> Understanding the similarities and differences between positive and negative reinforcement will set the stage for a conversation about selecting and using reinforcers with students in your classroom as a part of your management system.

being responsible in your classroom]). In a compatible yet contrasting manner, *negative reinforcement* is the removal of an undesired stimulus on the performance of a desired behavior in order to increase the likelihood of future recurrence of that same desired behavior. For example, if a teacher needs to escort a student from class to class because he or she is having problems during class transitions, then once the student shows improved behavior, the teacher can stop escorting the student presuming that the student prefers to not be escorted by the teacher.

On positive and negative reinforcement

It is important for all of us as teachers to understand the similarities and differences between positive and negative reinforcement as noted previously. Another simple (and more personal) example may help to clarify the difference between these forms of reinforcement. I have three kids at home: Megan is 18 and soon off to college, Kevin is 16 and getting ready for his junior year in high school, and Kelsey—our youngest—is 13 (going on 21 in her mind's eye). With his permission, I will use a situation with Kevin to further illustrate the differences between positive and negative reinforcement. One of the expectations that my wife and I have established with Kevin is that he keep his room reasonably picked up (like many parents, we struggle with this issue on a somewhat regular basis). One way that we have operationally defined this expectation is that I need to be able to walk from one end of his room to the other without stepping on clothes or shoes, empty drink bottles, dumbbells and wrist weights, video games, or other forms of debris. Now, in light of this expectation, it is possible for me to get Kevin to pick up things off of his floor at home on a scheduled basis through frequent verbal reminders (usually identified by Kevin as "nagging"). If this becomes the predominant way in which I get him to comply with this expectation, however, then he may comply in the short run (at that given moment in time), but I may undercut my rapport over the long run as a result of being increasingly viewed as a "nag." Conversely, if I reinforce Kevin on a regular basis when I find that his room is picked up, or after a simple modeling prompt in the form of me picking up a shirt while I am talking with him about other things and in response he starts to pick up other things off the floor, then Kevin engages in the desired behavior in a more self-directed manner. Bottom line— positive reinforcement (in a general sense) is the more constructive way to go in terms of reinforcement.

============
Bottom line positive reinforcement (in a general sense) is the more constructive way to go in terms of reinforcement.
============

Now, make no mistake about it, both positive and negative reinforcement procedures are just that, reinforcement procedures. In other words, negative reinforcement is not punishment. Rather, both forms of reinforcement have the result of increasing the likelihood of desired behavior. Positive reinforcement, however, is the predominant procedure to employ in your classroom for a number of reasons. Most important, it increases the likelihood of desired behavior in a way that also helps you to build and maintain rapport with your students. In other words, much like my

============

You do not want to
jeopardize or trade
off your rapport to
simply see dull
compliance in the
short run as a
result of using nega-
tive reinforcement
on a regular or
increasing basis
(which can become
a very slippery
slope).

============

example with Kevin, you do not want to jeopardize or trade off your rapport to simply see dull compliance in the short run as a result of using negative reinforcement on a regular or increasing basis (which can become a very slippery slope). Used sparingly and interspersed with a lot of positive reinforcement, negative reinforcement can be useful, but it should come with a warning label that advises all of us to use it with extreme caution.

Having noted the relationship between positive and negative reinforcement, it is important to identify things such as praise, privileges and attention that your students enjoy, given that positive reinforcement is really the name of the classroom management game. First consider the reinforcing nature of your time and attention, as this is readily at your disposal. By this, I am not suggesting that attention is a universal reinforcer that will work with each student in all situations. Rather, what I am suggesting is that you will likely find that your attention will serve as one of your most easily acceptable and (perhaps) powerful forms of reinforcement. The key to selecting reinforcers is figuring out your students' interests. Some kids respond well to public praise for performance and other kids respond well to private praise, whereas others may respond better to a combination of public and private praise. The challenge comes in understanding your students and figuring out what makes each one tick (so to speak). You will likely find that acknowledging appropriate behavior in the form of praise is a relatively cost-effective form of reinforcement that you can easily use on a daily basis in your classroom. You can always build in additional systematic forms of reinforcement in your classroom (e.g., use of tangible slips of paper or coupons in the form of a token economy) as the nature of your classroom and your teaching style urges you. Even in such instances, however, it is essential to pair explicitly clear and precise verbal praise that makes clear the student and action that are being acknowledged along with other forms of naturally occurring reinforcers with the delivery of other types of less naturally occurring reinforcers (e.g., coupons, tokens) for appropriate student behavior.

============

Acknowledging appropriate behavior in the form of praise is a relatively cost-effective form of reinforcement that you can easily use on a daily basis in your classroom.

============

One of the more common uses of reinforcement procedures involves applying the *Premack Principle*, in which access to a desired stimulus is made contingent on the appropriate use of a less desired stimulus in such a manner that the likelihood of increased appropriate use of the less desired stimulus becomes more predictable over time. Another way of stating this same principle of practice is that a more probable activity can be used to reinforce a less probable activity.

Given this definition of the Premack Principle, do you feel confident enough in your understanding to start to apply it in your classroom on a daily basis? Your initial reaction to the previous descriptions of the Premack Principle may be similar to my initial reaction when a mentor exposed me to these same descriptions (i.e., "What a bunch of gobbledy gook. Why can't people just say things in plain language?"). The

============
The Premack Principle, although important, is nothing more than having an understanding that in life sometimes you have to do one thing in order to gain access to another.
============

previous definition, although technically accurate, does little to help you gain a practical understanding of this important concept. Perhaps a more user-friendly way to define (for understanding) this principle of practice is to rename it the "Meal Time Rule." The "Meal Time Rule" is familiar to parents and children alike: "You can have dessert after you eat all of your vegetables." The Premack Principle, although important, is nothing more than having an understanding that in life sometimes you have to do one thing (that is not necessarily something you enjoy doing for its own sake, such as eating your vegetables) in order to gain access to another (that which you prefer, such as dessert). Now, some may say this is nothing more than bribery and that it is manipulative in nature. I guess in a narrow sense it is, but if this is true, then so too is much of life because gaining access to things that we prefer is often somewhat contingent on our performance of other things (e.g., as much as I enjoy teaching, I do get a paycheck every 2 weeks that I highly value). The reality is that the Premack Principle is in play each and every day for each of us in our lives. In other words, it is not just something that is used by you (or me) as a teacher, but it is also a part of everyday life for each and every one of us because we have all had varying degrees of experience with this principle of reinforcement. Beyond the "Meal Time Rule," Table 6.1 provides examples of the Premack Principle in action.

Now, with your current understanding about the principle of reinforcement (and the nature of reinforcers), let's turn our attention to the pragmatics of

Table 6.1. Examples of the Premack Principle in everyday life

Less desired behavior	More desired behavior
If you share your toys with others	Then others will be more likely to share their toys with you
If you appropriately say please, thank you, and I am sorry	Then you will increase your number of friends in the classroom
If you organize and complete your assigned work promptly	Then you will earn higher grades and associated privileges
If you consistently come home by curfew	Then you can stay out until 11:00 p.m. on the weekend
If you consistently drive responsibly	Then you may have access to the family car when needed
As a person in a relationship, if you will simply be still and listen (as opposed to trying to solve the problem) when your significant other is going off (sharing) about something that upset him or her that day at work	Then _____ (I am confident that you can fill in this blank)

using reinforcement in your classroom on a regular basis. One common misunderstanding about reinforcing student behavior is that many teachers feel that in order to be fair, everyone should get the same amount of reinforcement (e.g., number of instances of verbal praise, high fives, or the delivery of tokens). Simply put, fairness does not always mean that everyone gets the same thing at the same time. Rather, fairness really means (especially in the learning process within your classroom) that everyone gets what they need with the understanding that needs will vary from student to student and that these needs change over time and across different situations. To help you understand this point, I will

============
Fairness really means that everyone gets what they need with the understanding that needs will vary from student to student and that these needs change over time and across different situations.
============

paraphrase Dr. Richard Lavoie (presenter of the F.A.T. [Frustration, Anxiety, and Tension] City workshop) through the following illustration.

On fairness Suppose that I am providing an in-service at a local school when, suddenly, a teacher by the name of Joan slumps over in her chair, falls to the floor in full cardiac arrest, and appears to have stopped breathing. How ludicrous would it be if I said, "Joan, I would really like to help you out here. I mean, I know CPR and first aid. In fact, as a teacher, I am certified in it. I could save your life, but I just don't have time to give everyone in the classroom CPR or mouth-to-mouth resuscitation. It just wouldn't be fair for me to give it to you and not to the rest of these nice folks in attendance here today. So although I don't like it anymore than you do, I guess you are on your own." To reiterate: fairness does not always mean that everyone gets the same thing at the same time. Rather, fairness really means (especially in the learning process within your classroom) that everyone gets what they need with the understanding that needs will vary from student to student and that these needs change over time and across different situations.

Another way to think about differences of need in your classroom in terms of reinforcement (and your ability to differentiate your use of reinforcement to meet each of your student's needs) is through the following analogy. Differentiating reinforcement procedures between students is like differentiating your eating patterns based on your level of hunger. I mean, you and I eat (in general) only when we are hungry (with perhaps the exception of holiday gluttony). For example, let's say you and a friend of yours are attending my in-service training. You have just come from lunch where you were able to order your favorite food from a local eatery, and you are stuffed. Another friend, however, missed lunch today due to an appointment. So I kindly offer her some peanut butter crackers. I do not offer you the same. As long as you don't feel that my

============
What is reinforcing at a given moment in time is relative to the person being reinforced.
============

failure to offer you some crackers was mean spirited in nature, it's unlikely that you're going to get too upset that your colleague was offered something to eat and you were not because you currently feel full and you know your friend is hungry. Your friend has a need for food at this moment in time, whereas you do not. This doesn't mean that you will never be hungry again. Rather, you simply are not hungry at this time. Thinking about differentiating your practice of reinforcement in this way can be very useful in that 1) it helps you to understand that what is reinforcing at a given moment in time is relative to the person being reinforced and 2) it can be liberating (as a teacher) to understand that the goal is not to deliver the exact same amount of reinforcement (e.g., verbal praise) from student to student as if you were a human candy dispenser or gumball machine.

Now, given what I have shared with you thus far about reinforcement, and in particular, positive reinforcement, you have to be thinking, "So how do I figure out what is the right amount of reinforcement to provide to my students? I mean, in a practical sense, how do I make this work in my classroom?" Well, first, I encourage you to understand that there is not some preset number of times that reinforcement should be delivered on any given day and to think about your reinforcement procedures in terms of what I like to describe as a range of proportionality. By this I mean that you want to aim to provide four instances of positive reinforcement for any given student's appropriate social behavior for every one time you find yourself giving that same student corrective feedback for problem behavior. In other words, this is what is meant by the infamous 4:1 ratio in the field. Now, in this sense, everyone gets access to the same thing (this 4:1 ratio). What is different from student to student may be the time interval within which the 4:1 ratio is achieved on the basis of each student's needs.

On gauging students' needs

Let's say you have three particular kids in your classroom who, for a variety of reasons in your own mind's eye, are increasingly becoming distant from you (despite your efforts to increase rapport-building opportunities with each of them). In a parallel sense you find yourself correcting problem behavior with each of these three kids to a greater extent than the rest of your class. Let's say Jane seems to warrant corrective feedback from you once daily, Carlos about twice as often (on average once in the morning and once every afternoon), and Jimmy requires corrective feedback once every class period (six to eight times per day). So, what does this 4:1 ratio look like with these three kids in concert with all of the other students in your classroom? Simply use your instincts with each student in question, coupled with your expertise and understanding about the principle of reinforcement, including this issue of proportionality and the 4:1 ratio. You know based on current levels of behavioral performance that you have a reasonably long period of time to catch the bulk of your kids in your classroom on their best behavior. In other words, their low or even nonexistent level of problem behavior grants you a larger block of time within which to provide reinforcement for expected behavior. Now, in general it wouldn't hurt to reinforce the others in your classroom for prosocial behavior on a more frequent basis, but the point is that you have the luxury of more time with most of your kids based on their current levels of performance. The time interval for Jane is a bit more prescribed in that her daily rate of problem behavior suggests that you may have up to no more than a full day within which to catch Jane doing things the right way on at least four occasions. Carlos, based on his needs, has a tighter time interval in that you need to have him on your radar screen four times in the morning and four times in the afternoon by catching him doing things the correct way. Jimmy, based on his pattern of behavioral need, will require you to systematically attend to him in order to catch him doing things the correct way four times each class period in order to constructively prevent problem behavior over the longer term and yes, for the record, Jimmy appears to be "high maintenance kid."

============
Appropriate behavior by your other kids who have been behaviorally successful is likely to continue to occur as long as they feel they are being acknowledged in a manner that is meaningful.
============

This type of differentiation in your professional practice is based on student need, not preference (per se) on your part. In other words, you are not favoring one student over another; you are professionally differentiating your instructional practice based on your understanding of your students' needs. What is consistent is achieving the targeted 4:1 ratio with each of your students; what varies is the time interval within which you are working based on the level of your students' needs.

Will the other kids who are not getting as frequent attention as Jane, Carlos, and Jimmy rebel? Well, it really depends on your ability to meet each of their needs for acknowledgment on an ongoing basis. Yes, those other kids will likely rebel (in various forms) if your proportionality of reinforcement does not continue to adequately address each of their needs for acknowledgment. In other words, if another kid begins to feel like he or she is being taken for granted, then you are likely to see more frequent nuisance (and perhaps problem) behavior from him or her. This simply means you may need to shorten the time interval for reinforcement of appropriate behavior for that particular student. Think back to the food analogy that I previously shared. Appropriate behavior by your other kids who have been (at least to date) behaviorally successful is likely to continue to occur as long as they feel they are being acknowledged in a manner that is meaningful. Sure, occasionally you may have one particular student who begins to voice his or her displeasure in a manner that may require you to pull that student aside and talk privately with him or her as to your expectations in this regard. As long as each of your students (in a general sense) feels as if he or she is acknowledged at a reasonable level—as viewed from his or her perspective—significant problems in this regard are unlikely to surface. All of your kids need reinforcement; however, not all will need reinforcement at the same exact time. The key is finding the 4:1 ratio with each of your students.

This notion of the 4:1 ratio, by the way, is not an arbitrary number or concept. It is based on practical experiences in terms of what has been proven to be effective. Specifically, this 4:1 ratio reflects the similar notion of proportionality as the 80%–20% split of prevention to intervention. To help you put into practice this idea of proportionality, I have provided in the Appendix descriptions of simple self-monitoring procedures relevant to achieving this 4:1 ratio in your classroom. I encourage you to consider using one of these (or another similar approach) to periodically self-monitor your reinforcement practices within your classroom.

Now, given that you have a working sense of the importance (and power) of reinforcement, it is important to select appropriate reinforcers to use with your students. Earlier I noted that what any one particular student will find reinforcing is going to be relative to him or her (e.g., public verses private praise). Therefore, you may find it helpful to identify additional things (besides your attention) that your students find desirable. You can then utilize this information in the process of providing positive reinforcement to your students for desired behavior. There are many different ways to approach identifying potential reinforcers for use in your classroom. The most important thing to understand is that there is no clear set of universal reinforcers—in other words, no one size fits all. Remember, what works with one student may not work with another. Table 6.2 provides four commonly used approaches to identify reinforcers for use with particular students in your classroom.

In the previous three chapters, we have looked at prevention strategies to 1) build rapport, 2) establish behavioral expectations, and 3) enhance student behavioral performance through positive reinforcement. I would urge you to view each of these three aspects of classroom management as linked with the other two components. Although each of these principles of practice is important in its own right, each is exponentially strengthened when implemented in concert with its counterparts. Much like a three-legged stool, in which no one leg balancing by itself can match the degree of strength and stability it contributes to the assembled piece of furniture, these components of classroom management are each rendered more effective when used together. This system of prevention can help you establish a conducive learning environment and subsequently a welcoming classroom climate for everyone. So, although each of these three principles by themselves are of

Table 6.2.   Common approaches to identifying reinforcers

Strategy	Description
Watch and learn	Start by observing your students during situations in which they have freedom of choice in activities and with whom they interact. In other words, to paraphrase Yogi Berra, you can see a lot by looking. Gain a sense of the things (stimuli) that your kids find enjoyable based on the choices that they exercise during situations such as free time, recess, and other nonacademic settings and routines.
Reinforcer inventory	Create a list of potential reinforcers in the format of a checklist and/or questionnaire. Use a Likert-type scale (e.g., 1 to 5, with 1 being least desired and 5 being most desired) when developing the inventory. Then have your students independently complete the inventory and review the results to gain insight into what they report. Remember that what is reported on an inventory is not always consistent with what that person may actually do in real-life situations. Therefore, some of your students may simply respond by reporting things that they think you want them to say in terms of their respective responses.
Interview students	Sit down and talk with your students (or their parents) in groups and/or one to one. Ask them about the types of things that make them feel good and/or proud, as well as the types of things that would represent their worst nightmare (in terms of the classroom). As with inventories, remember that verbal self-report (like written self-report) is not as reliable or accurate a measure as actually seeing what someone does (remember the old proverb of "do as I say and not as I do").
Best guess, trial and error	Think about the ages and cultural backgrounds of your students. Specifically, what types of things are other students of similar age and backgrounds into in terms of activities of choice. Try some of these in the classroom (combine with "watch and learn"), and use the process of elimination to identify the most powerful reinforcers that you can use on a menu of options.

============

Much like a three-legged stool, in which no one leg balancing by itself can match the degree of strength and stability it contributes to the assembled piece of furniture, these components of classroom management are each rendered more effective when used together.

============

value to you as a teacher, it is in viewing these practices collectively that can best help you to nurture a culture of behavioral competence with your students and—to revisit the perspective of Haim Ginott (1972)—create fair weather for learning within your classroom. The whole is worth more than the sum of its parts, as the interactive effect among these principles of practice can help you to establish a classroom climate conducive for learning.

So Does It Really Boil Down to Classroom Climate?

Does classroom management really boil down to classroom climate? In a word, yes. How is that for brevity—that is, if we agree that classroom climate is a reflection of our classroom's culture as it relates to the shared belief systems, norms, and rituals that are present on a daily basis? Look, make no mistake about it, terms such as *learning environment*, *learning atmosphere*, *classroom ecology*, and *educational milieu* are used in the field to talk with one another about our perceptions of the nature of our classrooms (i.e., classroom climate). Perceptions are funny things to understand, however. Perception is a highly personalized experience, and, in many ways, much like opinion because our perceptions can become our own reality. This is not necessarily a good or bad thing. It just is and therefore is something to be aware of as our perceptions do affect how we think

===========
An overreliance on formal information (systematic data) as a prerequisite to form opinion can freeze you like a deer in the headlights of a fast approaching car.
===========

and act on a daily basis (including how each of us acts in the classroom). This is one of the reasons why it is helpful to inform our opinions (and thus influence our perceptions) with formal information or data (e.g., our anecdotal notes, including discipline referrals) from which we can draw insight into the situations we encounter. You will likely find, however, that an overreliance on formal information (systematic data) as a prerequisite to form opinion can freeze you like a deer in the headlights of a fast approaching car. Suffice it to say, when it comes to classroom management, I am a firm believer in the value of *both* your gut impressions of your classroom climate coupled with using a reasonable amount of formal data.

It is important and necessary to collect some data to inform your impression of classroom climate and meet the requirements of national and state standards. Having said this, I want to be very clear that I highly discourage blind worship at the proverbial altar of science for science's sake in the form of data collection, especially in this era of high-stakes testing in which we are increasingly compelled to collect data for (what at least on occasion appears as) data's sake.

On gut impressions

I remember a brief encounter that I had with a good friend and colleague of mine some time ago that has stuck with me to this day. I think, in his own gentle way, he was trying to remind me that although scientific data can be useful, it is woefully inadequate by itself to really capture the essence of the human experience. One day, in preparation for an in-service training, we were talking about the use of data in making instructional decisions, and during a lull in the discussion, he asked me how my recent summer vacation was with my family. After I related my experience about our family trip to the shore, he asked me if I had any pictures, which seemed normal but odd as he knew me well enough to know that I am not a big picture taker. In response, I said, "No. Well, a couple, but nothing that really capture the nature of the trip." To which he said, "How do you know? I mean, how do you know if you had a good time if you don't have any pictures—that is to say that you have no hard data—to support your claim? What you really have shared with me is simply your perspective with no substantiation as to how you reached that conclusion." To this I replied (and please remember that I knew this colleague very well), "Wise guy, I hate it when you prove me wrong!" Now, I share this not to negate the value of data (in this example, pictures or other forms of keepsakes from our trip). Rather, my point is that your gut impressions, more times than not, do capture the essence of your personal experiences, whether it be your perspective of your family vacation or the climate in your classroom.

I am a proponent of collecting and using data. After all, I am a part of the academic community and to say anything to contrary may be viewed as heresy!

============
We can significantly influence our classroom climate and therefore the subsequent gut impressions of our students (and for ourselves) as a result of implementing the three primary aspects of preventative classroom management—rapport, expectations, and reinforcement.
============

A teacher's collection and analysis of data can be valuable in the classroom, especially when it comes to designing, implementing, and evaluating the impact of student-centered interventions and supports such as the type I briefly discuss in Chapter 8. For example, collecting data in the form of monitoring your own use of reinforcement produces for appropriate behavior as compared with your use of redirection procedures in response to student problem behavior can be invaluable. You are encouraged to self-monitor on a periodic basis focusing on two levels (or units of analysis): 1) your class of students in aggregate and 2) specific, individual students who appear at-risk for developing serious problem behavior.

Having said this, though, both we and our students will naturally develop perceptions (a gut sense) as to the nature of the learning environment that we establish within our classroom. We can significantly influence our classroom climate and therefore the subsequent gut impressions of our students (and for ourselves) as a result of implementing the three primary aspects of preventative classroom management—rapport, expectations, and reinforcement. In other words, the proof will be in the taste of the pudding in that we will not have to wait for the pictures (or test scores) to come back to determine the learning climate of our classroom.

In a related manner, in corporate America (specifically the area of organizational management), a direct, positive correlation between worker morale and productivity exists. This is compatible with employees' perspectives (their collective gut sense, so to speak) that they will do better work if they are working in environments that are conducive to meeting their needs as well as meeting the bottom line for their employer. Likewise, as teachers we can anticipate higher levels of student academic and behavioral achievement when our students feel they are working in environments that are conducive to meeting their needs as well as meeting the bottom line, which is measured by many indicators of student achievement. Specifically, educational research in tandem with everyday teacher perspectives suggests more than just a casual relationship between classroom climate, student morale, and achievement. Furthermore, the issue of classroom climate has been linked with teacher morale and shown similar effects as noted in corporate America with respect to teacher satisfaction and burnout. This should not come as a surprise when we consider that all members of the classroom community have a vested interest—a shared stake, so to speak—in the feel of the classroom. As such, each member of the classroom (each student and you as the teacher) in his or her own way makes a contribution to the classroom's climate. The contribution by you as the teacher goes beyond your natural role as the classroom leader and includes you as a part of the learning community with your classroom. Simply stated, the more your students are well behaved, the happier you will be. In turn, the happier you are, the happier and more suc-

=============
As teachers, we can anticipate higher levels of student academic and behavioral achievement when our students feel they are working in environments that are conducive to meeting their needs as well as meeting the bottom line, which is measured by many indicators of student achievement.
=============

cessful your students will likely be both now and in the future.

Establishing a healthy classroom climate is not only useful in terms of the overall classroom management plan but also sets the stage for time-efficient and effective individualization with certain students as I have described in Chapter 8. For example, remember Jimmy from Chapter 6? Arguably, Jimmy creates a challenge with which any classroom teacher can identify. Jimmy's level of problem behavior has reached a point at which it is increasingly clear that continuing the exact same approach that has been employed to date will likely only result in the same types of problems. In other words, you may find yourself increasingly redirecting problem behavior and, as a result, really struggling with achieving the 4:1 ratio that I described in Chapter 6. Jimmy is a classic example of a youngster who creates the need for you to start to bridge the gap between your group-management procedures (in the form of your general classroom management) and student-centered programming.

Establishing a behavior contract is a logical first step toward developing a student-centered approach to working with Jimmy. It is important to establish a contract that will work with Jimmy in a way that is also compatible with your system of classroom management. If a contract proves insufficient, in tandem with continuation of your preventative approaches to classroom management, then the next logical step would be to conduct an initial (or entry-

level) functional behavior assessment (FBA) and subsequently design a student-centered behavior
intervention plan based on the results of the
functional behavior assessment. In other
words, additional student-centered approaches can be explored when a student,
for whatever reason(s), appears to respond
insufficiently to your classroom management plan.

An important thing to understand is
that every teacher experiences a given student
here or there along the way whose behavioral
pattern mirrors Jimmy's. This is not necessarily a sign of failure on your part (given,
of course, that you have put into place the
principles of practice highlighted in previous chapters). Rather, this is simply a reflection of the degree of diversity that we have in our
schools today. Having said this, by implementing the
preventative approaches that I have highlighted in
previous chapters, you will be in a good position to
work effectively and efficiently with students such as
Jimmy. More specifically, having established a conducive classroom climate for learning should prove
beneficial to you in your work with Jimmy (regardless
of the presence or absence of a disability) as well as
other students with similarly complicated behavioral
histories. What this means with respect to Jimmy is
that you should find implementing the student-
centered interventions and supports highlighted in the
next chapter more manageable if you already have in
place the principles of practice that I have described
in previous chapters. In a more direct sense, your
classroom will be a welcoming place in which you can
reasonably address Jimmy's needs in a way that

enables you to 1) continue to succeed with your other students, 2) experience increasing success with Jimmy through student-centered approaches, and 3) maintain your sanity in the process.

8

So **What Else Can I Do?**

Understandably, you must be thinking, "Where do I turn next in working with Jimmy and any other students that do not seem to sufficiently respond to my approach to classroom management?" Well, for starters, don't panic. You should find that the preventative approaches that we have focused on should work sufficiently well with most of your students. There will be a given student along the way, however, who will require more student-centered (specific) intervention and support in tandem with continued implementation of your classroom management plan. There are logical next steps (or levels of intervention) to consider and actions to take in order to sufficiently individualize your approach with Jimmy (and other students) as needed.

There are three levels of intervention to consider in your endeavors to individualize your approach with Jimmy. Interventions within each level are presented in Table 8.1. I will briefly describe this continuum of student-centered interventions to provide you with initial guidance in this regard. Having said this, it is important to remember that the primary focus of this

Table 8.1. Continuum of levels of student-centered interventions

Level	Descriptor	Interventions
Level 1	Indirect intervention	Planned ignoring in individual and group situations for responding to nuisance behavior
	Direct intervention	Stop, redirect, and reinforce procedures for responding to problem behavior
Level 2	Behavior contracting	To be employed to further augment your student-centered approach when problem behavior persists despite your 1) attempts to increase your use of preventative procedures in tandem with 2) use of Level 1 intervention described above
	Mentoring	
Level 3	Behavior intervention plan based on a functional behavior assessment (FBA)	To be employed to further augment student-centered precision when problem behavior persists after implementation of a behavior contract. The steps involved include 1. Conducting the FBA 2. Summarizing results of the FBA into hypotheses 3. Designing and implementing the behavior intervention plan 4. Monitoring student progress 5. Modifying the plan as warranted over time

book (as highlighted in Chapters 1–7) is on preventative classroom management. As such, it is equally important for you to realize that you may (likely) need to refer to additional resources to gain a more comprehensive understanding of the interventions described in this chapter because they highlight approaches in response to increasing degrees of problem behavior. I have provided a few good starting points for you along these same lines in the Appendix.

In addressing the initial level of intervention (response) to inappropriate behavior, let me reiterate a point that I described in Chapter 3 concerning undesirable behavior. It is important to differentiate between nuisance behavior and problem behavior as each warrants a different type of response. As the old saying goes, you do not want to make a mountain out of a mole hill (i.e., overreact to nuisance-level behavior). But you also do not want minor waves in your classroom pool to become tsunamis (i.e., nuisance behavior escalating into significant problem behavior). Furthermore, it is important to remember that how you respond to both nuisance and problem behavior will take place within the context of your overall approach to classroom management (i.e., the preventative principles of practice we have been looking at thus far).

As a reminder, nuisance behaviors are the things that kids do that alone are inconsequential. These behaviors can also really wear you down over time in the classroom. For example, frequent minor occurrences of off-task behavior with a particular student or group of students can really get on your nerves. Nuisance (inconsequential) behavior is best addressed through indirect intervention—thus, not calling attention to the student while he or she is engaged in the nuisance behavior (or "junk" behavior [Latham, 1999]). There are generally two ways in which you can systematically ignore nuissance behav-

====================
Nuisance (inconsequential) behavior is best addressed through indirect intervention.
====================

ior. One way is to simply not respond to Jimmy's nuisance behavior during a one-to-one situation with him. Rather, focus on things that he is doing correctly and avoid feeding into his inappropriate behavior (e.g., fidgeting, perseverations, brief moments of off-task behavior). The second way to ignore nuissance behavior can be used when Jimmy engages in inappropriate behavior in a group setting. Simply find other 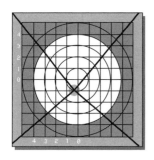 students who are engaged in appropriate behavior who are in close physical proximity to Jimmy. Keep Jimmy on your radar screen in a way that does not suggest to Jimmy that you are watching him. Reinforce those other students one at a time for appropriate behavior and do not respond to Jimmy's nuissance behavior. Reinforce Jimmy for appropriate behavior once he ceases the nuissance behavior. In both situations, the key strategy is that you want to ignore the nuisance behavior. Don't feed into it. Use the same reinforcement procedures that were described in Chapter 6 for appropriate behavior. Using this approach to indirectly respond to inconsequential behavior should help to position you to act in a manner consistent with the preventative approaches that have been previously highlighted.

Inappropriate behavior ceases to be inconsequential when the behavior of concern persists for an unacceptable amount of time (e.g., Jimmy being off task for longer than you view as reasonable despite your efforts to indirectly intervene as described previously) or when the behavior of concern becomes disruptive or potentially harmful (e.g., pulling other kids off task, creating an unsafe situation). When problem behavior occurs, you should directly intervene employing a basic three-step process: 1) tell Jimmy to stop the problem behavior (e.g., name calling, being out of his seat, interrupting classmates), 2) direct Jimmy to an appropriate behavior, and 3) reinforce Jimmy once he complies with your redirection. To be clear, you are not reinforcing Jimmy for the problem behavior. Rather, you are reinforcing Jimmy for compliance with your redirection. (Be sure to be explicit about what you are reinforcing by labeling your praise).

> ===============
> When using a redirection procedure, keep your words and actions to a minimum, thus allowing you to be time efficient while observing how the student responds.
> ===============

When using a redirection procedure, keep your words and actions to a minimum, thus allowing you to be time efficient while observing how the student (Jimmy in this situation) responds. Furthermore, keeping your words and actions to a minimum reduces the likelihood of getting drawn into long conversations (at least at this point in time) and will also make you less susceptible to what is referred to as "bait and switch" tactics at which some students become masterful (e.g., the student placing blame elsewhere, making accusations of being picked on or singled out by you; other things that enable the student to switch your focus from the issue at hand). Table 8.2 outlines a basic three-part script that I encourage you to consider when using redirection procedures.

Now, if you find yourself increasingly using redirection procedures with Jimmy—despite your logical efforts to increase your use of preventative procedures—you also may be struggling to achieve

Table 8.2.   Three-part script to redirect a given student's problem behavior

Step in process	What to say
Part 1 In the instance in which Jimmy engages in problem behavior, you want to directly intervene by getting in close physical proximity and assertively stopping him from continuing in the problem behavior.	Represent the problem behavior, be specific, and label the problem behavior (e.g., "Jimmy, stop grabbing John's materials off his desk").
Part 2 Once you have gained Jimmy's attention with your "stop" statement, you will redirect Jimmy to an alternative behavior that is in keeping with your expectations.	Represent the alternative behavior (e.g., "Keep your hands on your own materials and start doing your work").
Part 3 Once you have redirected Jimmy, you will pause and wait for him to respond. If Jimmy does not comply, then simply repeat your verbal redirection, adding additional prompts and cues to enable student compliance. Once compliance occurs, provide reinforcement for following your redirection.	Provide explicit verbal praise for compliance (e.g., "Thank you Jimmy for using your own materials and doing your work").

the 4:1 ratio of reinforcement to corrective feedback that was described in Chapter 6. Establishing a behavior contract is a logical next step under such circumstances and represents the second level of intervention to further individualize your approach with Jimmy.

There are two important things to keep in mind when developing a behavior contract. First, the primary goal of a behavior contract is to see sufficient improvement in behavior so that you can wean the student (e.g., Jimmy) off the contract within a reasonable amount of time. Second, at its very core, a behavior contract is nothing more than a systematic, student-centered way of further defining behavioral expectations and increasing the likelihood of being able to catch Jimmy doing things the correct way. An effective contract should enable you to reinforce Jimmy at a more sufficient rate based on his performance (thus, behavior contracts are consistent with the principle of reinforcement that I emphasized in Chapter 6). This is typically accomplished by further operationally defining the same behavioral expectations that you have for all of your students while also establishing a clear criterion for performance within a reasonable (typically shorter) time interval for that given student. In short, an effective behavior contract has more to do with reinforcement procedures than it has to do with negative consequences (given, of course, that you select meaningful reinforcement procedures for the student in question). Examples of behavior contracts are provided in the Appendix for your review.

> A behavior contract is nothing more than a student-centered way of defining behavioral expectations and increasing the likelihood of being able to catch students doing things the correct way.

An additional strategy to consider at this second level of intervention is to establish some form of mentor program with the particular student of concern. Connecting the student with an adult of his or her preference in the school to provide periodic support and guidance can help to reduce problem behavior (e.g., student periodically touches base with his or her mentor each day for preventative purposes). Mentor programs may be used in tandem with behavior contracting.

Now, you must be thinking, "What if I find myself continuing to increase my use of systematic

====================
An effective
behavior contract
has more to do
with reinforcement
procedures than it
has to do with neg-
ative consequences.
====================

ignoring of nuisance behavior or, worse yet, find myself increasingly needing to stop and redirect Jimmy in response to increasing degrees of disruptiveness? What if all of my preventative approaches coupled with my use of systematic ignoring, stop and redirect tactics, and a behavior contract fails to sufficiently change Jimmy's behavior? Where do I turn and what do I do?" Well, all is not lost by any means. In fact, all of your efforts thus far with Jimmy have set the stage for the third level of intervention to further individualize your approach with Jimmy.

First and foremost, it is important to keep things in perspective and to remember that one of the keys to effectively intervening with Jimmy at this next level will be to understand why he engages in problem behavior. A functional behavior assessment (FBA) is the process of gathering information that can help you understand the reason for Jimmy's problem behavior. This assessment process is also the same FBA procedure that is required in the Individuals with Disabilities Education Improvement Act (IDEA) of 2004 (PL 108-446). Numerous published resources are available to you when you are conducting a comprehensive FBA. I will briefly describe the basic principles in conducting an initial (entry-level, or what is sometmes called intuitive) FBA here; however, you are encouraged to seek more in-depth reference materials (some of which are noted in the Appendix) when you find yourself needing to conduct a more in-depth, comprehensive FBA.

For starters, it is important to remember that behavior occurs within a context. In other words, Jimmy's behavior is connected to the classroom environment, and his problem behavior is not random in nature (even though it may feel as such to you). Furthermore, it is equally important to understand that behavior also serves a purpose, which is referred to as a *function*, for the student engaging in the behavior of concern. For example, let's say that Jimmy disrupts the class by making loud noises, saying derogatory comments, and repeatedly being off task and out of his seat—in other words, he is a real handful. You find that you can get him back on task and settle him down with some basic redirection procedures, but this is fast becoming an interactive dance that you appear to have with Jimmy very frequently. In fact, you are increasingly concerned that if this pattern persists, Jimmy will be spending significant portions of his school day in various forms of time-out (in your room as well as in the principal's office). Where do you start, and how do you progress with Jimmy should he continue to misbehave on a regular basis? Here is where understanding both *context and function* of a given student's problem behavior comes into play.

Although I have placed great emphasis on preventative approaches thus far, you will (of course) also need to respond to nuisance as well as problem behavior when it occurs (and with Jimmy, it most certainly is occurring). In other words, although you want to spend the majority of your time that you invest in classroom management on proactive approaches, you will also need to react to student

============
Understandably, you
will respond to
disruptive situations
with reactive
interventions that
have the intent of
reducing, or getting
rid of all together,
the problem behav-
ior of concern. This
is both logical and
the professionally
responsible thing
to do.
============

behavioral errors. Understandably, you will respond to such situations with reactive interventions that have the intent of reducing, or getting rid of all together, the problem behavior of concern. This is both logical and the professionally responsible thing to do. As teachers, however, we often can become blinded by the intent of our interventions to such a degree that it can hinder our ability to decode the nature (context and function) of a given student's problem behavior. Let's continue with the example of Jimmy. Say that you have been redirecting Jimmy when he engages in these problem behaviors by sending him to time-out in response to his increasing degree of disruptiveness with the hope that time-out would reduce, or get rid of, Jimmy's name calling, noise making, and overall off-task behavior. Despite your intent and hard work, the problem behavior has actually been increasing—just the opposite of what you intended. Jimmy is becoming increasingly "intervention resistant." In other words, he is not responding the way you want him to respond. Now, here is where keeping things in perspective becomes really important. Because of his increasingly bad behavior, you may start being less nurturing in your approach. This is a natural human response as you are becoming more frustrated with Jimmy and his behavior on many levels for many reasons. When we become frustrated, we ourselves become at risk to engage in (or continue with) interventions and approaches that make little sense in terms of making the situation better. In such instances, it is important to take a step back and try to interpret exactly how Jimmy is responding to your reactive interventions and to also try to decode patterns with respect to the occurrence as well as non-occurrence of Jimmy's problem behavior (e.g., Are there particular classes, times of the day, and/or situations in which Jimmy's behavior is better as well as worse?). One of the biggest hurdles for any teacher in decoding the reasons behind a given student's problem behavior is often a combination of our current reactive habits coupled with increasing degrees of frustration. In other words, our professional judgment is more likely to become clouded when we become upset at a given student's lack of response to our typical reactive approaches. Given the information that I shared with you back in Chapter 6 concerning Jimmy, it would appear that the use of time-out in response to his disruptiveness is not reducing or eliminating the problem behavior of concern. To the contrary, it actually appears that the use of time-out is associated with increasing levels of disruptiveness. As such, after reflecting on Jimmy's response to your interventions (including your use of time-out), it appears that Jimmy's disruptive behavior may, in fact, be motivated by escape. In other words, Jimmy becomes disruptive in order to escape the situation at hand (e.g., being sent to the time-out area, the hallway, or the office). Furthermore, it would appear that despite your intent to reduce Jimmy's problem behavior through your use of time-out, the use of your current time-out procedures may be actually reinforcing Jimmy's disruptive behavior. In other words, your

==============
Decoding the func-
tion(s) of a given
student's problem
behavior can help
you in the class-
room because it
makes the selection
and implementation
of interventions a
logical, systematic
process.
==============

typical response in the form of time-out to Jimmy's disruptiveness gives him what he wants: escape from the situation and/or the task at hand.

Just as professional intuition (i.e., your gut professional judgment as described in Chapter 7) is important to you in terms of classroom climate, it also is integral when conducting an initial (entry-level) FBA regarding Jimmy. The FBA process involves asking yourself a series of questions and capturing information that is relevant to your responses in order to form an educated guess or hypothesis as to the nature of Jimmy's disruptive behavior. Decoding behavior at this initial level through such informal and intuitive means represents the simplest form of FBA. You are then in a better position to select student-specific interventions that make sense with Jimmy based on your hypotheses (educated guesses) that summarize the results of this initial FBA.

Now, in this one example, it appears that the function of Jimmy's disruptive behavior was to escape/avoid the situation at hand. It is important to understand that although this was the function of Jimmy's problem behavior, there are a variety of reasons as to why any given student might act in a disruptive manner. Decoding the function(s) of a given student's problem behavior can help you in the classroom because it makes the selection and implementation of interventions a logical, systematic process. Minimizing the degree of random trial and error on your part by systematically creating educated guesses about the reason(s) behind Jimmy's problem behavior

Table 8.3. Examples of common consequences associated with specific functions

Function	Common consequences
Escape (to avoid something) After a problem behavior occurs, the student avoids something unpleasant or terminates a situation that he or she perceives as negative. The problem behavior may serve as an escape (avoidance) function if one of the following occurs.	The teacher provides assistance The task is made easier The student gets out of the task Use of time-out for problem behavior increases Performance demands are lessened Adults stop "nagging" Peers stop teasing The student is left alone
To get something (access to social interaction, preferred objects or events) After a problem behavior occurs, the student gets something that he or she desires. The problem behavior may serve to get something if one of the following occurs.	The student gets one-to-one teacher interaction or teacher contact increases The teacher verbally responds (even neutral or negative comments may be desired by the student) Peers respond by laughing Student gets more intense reactions The student is redirected to a more enjoyable activity The student gains access to things he or she wants (e.g., objects, activities, or other students) The student gets enjoyment/feels good as a result of engaging in the problem behavior

can help you to increasingly see desired behavior change in a time-efficient manner. Table 8.3 provides some examples of common consequences associated with specific functions of student problem behavior.

It is important to understand that the examples noted in Table 8.3 are just that—examples. Please do not misinterpret or overgeneralize these illustrations. In other words, determining the function of a given student's problem behavior is the result of conducting a student-centered FBA. Not all disruptive behavior by any given student will always serve the same function of escape/avoidance as was the case with Jimmy. Asking the core set of FBA questions helps you with decoding the nature of a given student's problem behavior. FBAs have been known to create a lot of stress for teachers in the field. Compounding this sense of angst is the reality that FBAs are often written in terms of legal requirements under IDEA (2004) or in professional journals that more typically look at empirical (scientific) studies with students with extreme forms of serious problem behavior. As important as it is to understand the legal requirements of conducting FBAs with students with disabilities, along with providing guidance to families and practitioners when working with students/clients with extreme forms of problem behavior, it's unfortunate that few publications emphasize more common, everyday applications of FBA procedures for classroom teachers. As such, let me distill for you the basics of conducting an initial (entry-level) FBA.

At its very root, an FBA is nothing more than a problem-solving process that reflects addressing a series of core questions regarding a given student and his or her problem behavior. You can gather information in many different ways when conducting an FBA. This variety of data-gathering procedures has (to some extent) added to the degree of confusion in the field about FBA. In other words, it can become difficult to see the forest (FBA) because of all of the trees (data-collection procedures). Having said this, I have found that teachers are best able to understand the assessment process by connecting the core questions associated with an FBA to other commonly used practices within their respective classrooms. For example, think about the basic approach to teaching comprehension of reading material within a classroom. Regardless of whether you are teaching young children to read for comprehension (in a general sense) or high school students to read for understanding a content area textbook, you look to engage your students by requiring them to think about questions to address as they read. Guiding your students to ask the infamous five "W" questions—who, what, when, where, and why—when they are reading is one commonly accepted approach when teaching for comprehension. In essence, conducting an initial (entry-level) FBA with a given student involves asking this same series of questions with an emphasis on his or her behavior. Table 8.4 presents a series of logical "W" questions to ask concerning Jimmy and his disruptive behavior.

Table 8.4.   Logical "W" questions

Context	Who is Jimmy with when he becomes disruptive?
	When is Jimmy's disruptive behavior most likely to occur? Are there particular circumstances when misbehavior is more likely?
	When is Jimmy's disruptive behavior least likely to occur?
	What is the nature of the routines and settings when Jimmy acts appropriately?
Behavior	What exactly does Jimmy do that is a problem?
	What does Jimmy look like and sound like when he is disruptive?
Consequence/function	Why does Jimmy engage in the problem behavior? What does he get or avoid as a result of being disruptive? What is the payoff for Jimmy?

Guiding your stu-
dents to ask the
infamous five "W"
questions—who,
what, when, where,
and why—when
they are reading is
one commonly
accepted approach
when teaching for
comprehension.

The reason for asking these questions in this sequence is to help you gain
an understanding as to why Jimmy
engages in disruptive behavior. Insight
in this regard can help you to select both
prevention and intervention approaches
that make sense to use with Jimmy. At a
conceptual level, an FBA helps you to
decode the series of events as well as to
decipher how each of those events relate
with one another in the antecedent-
behavior-consequence chain as depicted
in Figure 8.1.

Trigger "A"	Problem behavior "B"	Consequence "C"
Context	**Behavior**	**Function**
Who is the student with when he or she engages in the problem behavior?	What does the problem behavior look and sound like?	Why does the student engage in the problem behavior?
When is the student most likely to engage in problem behavior?		1. To escape or avoid something or some-one
When is the student most successful and therefore less likely to engage in the problem behavior?		2. To get something
Where does the student engage in the problem behavior, and are there other factors that might be contributing to the student's problem behavior?		What is the student saying (communicating) through the problem behavior?

Figure 8.1.   Antecedent-behavior-consequence chain.

The process of FBA also helps you identify triggers to problem behavior in addition to helping you decode the function of a given student's problem behavior (e.g., Jimmy's disruptiveness). Identifying triggers in this regard can help you to identify things that you can do in a very practical sense in your classroom that should help to minimize the likelihood that the student (e.g., Jimmy) will continue to be disruptive at the same level. Table 8.5 provides examples of common fast and slow triggers associated with problem behaviors that may be identified through an intuitive FBA process relevant to a given student's problem

============
Identifying triggers in this regard can help you to identify things that you can do in a very practical sense in your classroom that should help to minimize the likelihood that the student will continue to be disruptive at the same level.
============

Table 8.5.   Examples of common fast and slow triggers

General setting events (slow triggers)	Specific illness Poor diet, missed meals An upsetting experience earlier in the day Tired, poor night's sleep Limited opportunity for choice
Antecedents (fast triggers) commonly associated with escape and/or avoidance	Interruption of routines Transitions Lack of predictability Nonpreferred activity Difficult or repetitive work or task Boredom from easy work or task Too much work, overwhelmed
Antecedents (fast triggers) commonly associated with getting something (attention and /or objects and activities)	Access to a favorite object or activity is denied (often resulting in tantrums) Seeing someone else get attention Being unoccupied or unengaged Receiving low levels of attention Presence of a preferred person

behavior. You logically can make changes in your class-room procedures to address indicated triggers.

So there you have it! I have divulged to you highly sensitive trade secrets that are usually reserved for those who join the secret society of proverbial "behavior experts." Consider this book the closest thing you'll get to a secret decoder ring that unlocks the mysteries of student behavior. On a more serious note, I have shared some practical think-ing on a continuum of responses to problem behavior. With that said, this book does not exhaustively address all of the possible situations that may arise in your classroom. Please refer to the Appendix for addi-tional references on FBA and student-centered behav-ior intervention plans.

So How Do I Connect the Dots?

As I noted in Chapter 1, the primary focus of this book is on preventative class-room management. Given this emphasis, I have explored prevention through the three principles of practice described in earlier chapters and then progressed up through a cursory review of student-specific intervention related to problem be-havior. Effective classroom management is all about establishing a classroom climate that is conducive to learning for all of your students in a manner that allows you to see (and feel) positive, tangible results from your efforts. As I noted in Chapter 7, it really does boil down to classroom climate. A class-room climate conducive for learning is not something that just happens on its own, however. Rather, it develops over time as a result of thoughtful planning and action on the part of the classroom teacher. The key to making sense of all of this is to understand that

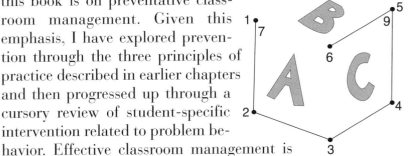

effective classroom management involves a variety of principles of practice that are employed in conjunction with one another. Also, please remember that the total (your classroom climate) becomes worth much more than simply the sum of its individual parts when the principles of 1) establishing rapport, 2) clearly defining behavioral expectations, and 3) reinforcing student performance of your behavioral expectations are employed in an integrated manner. Table 9.1 provides the highlights of these three interrelated principles of preventative practice.

Now, despite the prophylactic nature of these principles of practice and regardless of how thorough a job you do in implementing these preventative approaches, you will likely have a given student along the way who will require further individualization. It is important to remember that responding to problem behavior still reflects the basic tenants of preventative approaches emphasized in Chapters 2–8 of this book. When working with a student who has challenging behaviors, you are encouraged to increase your use of rapport-building strategies, teach and reteach your behavioral expectations, and endeavor to increase your frequency of reinforcing the student for both acquisition and fluency of socially expected behavior in your classroom. Furthermore, you are encouraged to consider the three levels of intervention highlighted in Chapter 8 in the instance in which student problem behavior persists despite your efforts to increase your use of preventative approaches. An overview of a continuum of practices to consider employing in response to increasing degrees of inappropriate behavior (ranging from nuisance to problem behavior) was also pro-

Table 9.1.   Three interrelated principles of preventative practice

Principle of practice	Description	Relationship to prevention
Establishing rapport	Rapport involves establishing and maintaining a trusting and caring relationship with each of your students. Rapport will naturally evolve between you and a number of your students. You will, however, have some students who appear harder to reach. It is particularly important to make a connection with these students. This is particularly the case if/when those same students who are at risk engage in undesired behavior.	The bottom line is that students will develop a higher degree of motivation to meet expectations for teachers with whom a trusting relationship has been established. Furthermore, student motivation in combination with maintaining rapport over time increases the likelihood of each of your students modeling expected behavior for their peers and best positions you to have greater opportunities to reinforce your students for meeting your expectations.
Defining behavioral expectations	Being clear about what you want your students to do helps you to establish a culture of behavioral competence within your classroom. Engage your students in defining the expectations across important settings and routines that naturally occur in your classroom. Have your students identify what they would "look like and sound like" when they are meeting your expectations.	It is essential for each of your students to be clear on what is expected, thus setting the stage for mastery (as opposed to mystery) learning. Clearly defining behavioral expectations creates the proverbial bull's eye for which your students will aim. Having clear expectations also operationally sets the stage for you to "catch your kids being good" in terms of reinforcement procedures.

(continued)

Table 9.1. *(continued)*

Principle of practice	Description	Relationship to prevention
Reinforcing student performance	Providing each of your students with sufficient acknowledgment (in various forms) for meeting behavioral expectations is essential to prevention of problem behavior. Although you will differentiate your frequency of reinforcement among your students, strive to achieve a 4:1 ratio of positive reinforcement for performance of expected behavior as compared with corrective feedback for undesirable behavior with each of your students.	The most efficient way to build appropriate behavior with your students is through reinforcing appropriate behavior on an ongoing basis. Effective use of reinforcement procedures makes the expectations you have identified become more tangible and come to life. Furthermore, being viewed by each of your students as someone who provides positive feedback will also further solidify your level of rapport with your students on an ongoing basis.

vided in Chapter 8. You are particularly encouraged to explore the additional references noted in the Appendix if you desire to learn more about conducting a comprehensive FBA (beyond the initial FBA that I have described) in order to design a student-centered behavior intervention and support plan. Implementation of the preventative approaches previously highlighted should help you realize success with most of your students and set the stage for time-efficient, student-centered behavior intervention and support. Last, and equally important, using these preventative practices should minimize the number of kids in your classroom whose behavior requires more student-centered intervention and therefore increase your personal degree of satisfaction with your job. After all, it is important to keep good teachers in our classrooms working with our children. Best of luck in all that you do.

============

Implementation of the preventative approaches previously highlighted should help you realize success with most of your students and set the stage for time-efficient, student-centered behavior intervention and support.

============

References and Resources for Further Reading

Albert, L. (1996). *Cooperative discipline.* Shoreview, MN: AGS Globe.

Alberto, P.C., & Troutman, A.C. (1999). *Applied behavior analysis for teachers* (5th ed.). Columbus, OH: Charles E. Merrill.

Bambara, L.M., & Kern, L. (2004). *Individualized supports for students with problem behaviors: Designing positive behavior plans.* New York: Guilford Press.

Bambara, L.M., & Knoster, T. (1998). *Designing positive behavior support plans.* Washington, DC: American Association on Intellectual and Developmental Disabilities.

Bambara, L.M., & Knoster, T. (2005). Designing positive behavior support plans. In M. Wehmeyer & M. Agran (Eds.), *Mental retardation and intellectual disabilities: Teaching students using innovative and research-based strategies* (pp. 149–174). Columbus, OH: Merrill/Prentice Hall.

Bruce, A. (2002). *Building a high morale workplace.* New York: McGraw-Hill.

Chafouleas, S., Riley-Tilman, T.C., & Sugai, G. (2007). *School-based behavioral assessment: Informing intervention and instruction.* New York: Guilford Press.

Crimmins, D., Farrell, A.F., Smith, P.W., & Bailey, A. (2007). *Positive strategies for students with behavior problems.* Baltimore: Paul H. Brookes Publishing Co.

Crone, D.A., & Horner, R.H. (2003). *Building positive behavior support systems in schools: Functional behavior assessment.* New York: Guilford Press.

Di Giulio, R.C. (2006). *Positive classroom management: A step-by-step guide to helping students succeed* (3rd ed.). Thousand Oaks, CA: Corwin Press.

Foster-Johnson, L., & Dunlap, G. (1993). Using functional assessment to develop effective, individualized interventions for challenging behaviors. *Teaching Exceptional Children, 25*(3), 44–50.

Gatto, J.T. (n.d.). *Underground history of American education: A schoolteacher's intimate investigation into the problem of modern schooling.* New York: The Odysseus Group.

Ginott, H.G. (1972). *Teacher and child: A book for parents and teachers.* New York: Macmillan.

Horner, R.H., Albin, R.W., Sprague, J.R., & Todd, A.W. (2000). Positive behavior support. In M.E. Snell & F. Brown (Eds.), *Instruction of students with severe disabilities* (5th ed.; pp. 207–243). Columbus, OH: Charles E. Merrill.

Horner, R.H., & Carr, E.G. (1997). Behavioral support for students with severe disabilities: Functional assessment and comprehensive intervention. *Journal of Special Education, 31*(1), 84–104.

Individuals with Disabilities Education Improvement Act (IDEA) of 2004, PL 108-446, 20 U.S.C. §§ 1400 *et seq.*

Jackson, L., & Panyan, M.V. (2001). *Positive behavioral support in the classroom: Principles and practices.* Baltimore: Paul H. Brookes Publishing Co.

Janney, R., & Snell, M.E. (2006). *Social relationships and peer support* (2nd ed.). Baltimore: Paul H. Brookes Publishing Co.

Knoster, T. (2003, January/February). Practical application of positive behavior support in schools: Understanding the basics of assessment, intervention, and support. *TASH Connections, 29*, 18–19.

Knoster, T., & McCurdy, B. (2002). Best practices in functional behavioral assessment for designing individualized student programs. In A. Thomas & J. Grimes (Eds.), *Best practices in school psychology* (Vol. IV; pp. 1007–1028). Bethesda, MD: National Association of School Psychologists.

Latham, G.I. (1999). *Parenting with love: Making a difference in a day.* Logan, UT: P&T Ink.

Rosen, P. (Producer/Director). (1996/1989). *Richard Lavoie: How difficult can this be?* The F.A.T. City Workshop [Video]. Washington, DC: Public Broadcasting Service.

Sundel, M., & Sundel, S.S. (2004). *Behavior change in the human services: Behavioral and cognitive principles and applications* (5th ed.). Thousand Oaks, CA: Sage Publications.

Thinkquest. (n.d.). *Discipline.* Retrieved January 28, 2008, from http://library.thinkquest.org/J002606/Discipline.html

WEB SITES

Association for Positive Behavior Support
http://www.apbs.org

Center on Positive Behavior Intervention and Support (CPBIS) funded by the U.S. Department of Education Office of Special Education Programs (OSEP)
http://www.pbis.org

Dr. Laura Riffle
http://www.behaviordoctor.org

Online Academy, University of Kansas
http://uappbs.apbs.org

Appendix

The Three Bees (Elementary School)

Expected Behavior (Middle School)

Performance Expectations (High School)

Strategies for Self-Monitoring the 4:1 Ratio in the Classroom

Behavior Contract

The Three Bees (Elementary School)

Expectation	Arrival at school	Individual work	Teacher talking	Group activities	Changing activities
Be ready	Go immediately to your classroom after arriving at school. Bring your homework with you to class. Be in your seat when the morning bell rings.	Have your materials open and on top of your desk. Follow directions the first time. Get to work right away.	Listen when Mrs. Lee speaks; one person speaks at a time. Write important things in your notebook.	Be focused on the group work to be completed. Have your materials with you and opened to assigned page. Organize your group and get to work quickly (within 1 minute).	Be aware of the daily schedule. Listen for directions from Mrs. Lee. Be flexible in case the schedule changes.
Be responsible	Be on time to school and class. Listen when Mrs. Lee speaks; one person speaks at a time. Complete your homework. Use indoor voices when speaking.	Follow directions on tests and assignments. Organize and get to work promptly. Make a good effort on all work. Speak only at appropriate times.	Think about what Mrs. Lee says. Ask Mrs. Lee questions by raising your hand. Volunteer to answer questions by raising your hand.	Focus on your work. One person speaks at a time using indoor voice. Ask for help as needed. Finish on time. Share with others while keeping your hands and feet to yourself.	Stop and put things away when Mrs. Lee says to do so. Know what materials you need for next class/activity. Keep your hands and feet to yourself. Use indoor voices when speaking.

(continued)

The Three Bees (Elementary School) *(continued)*

Expectation	Arrival at school	Individual work	Teacher talking	Group activities	Changing activities
Be respectful	Say "hi" to friends before homeroom starts. Keep hands and feet to yourself. Listen when Mrs. Lee speaks; one person speaks at a time. Follow directions the first time.	Get to work and work quietly. Use only your materials. Ask for help by raising hand. Make a good effort.	Listen and follow directions the first time. Think about what Mrs. Lee is saying. Ask questions by raising your hand. Volunteer to answer questions by raising your hand.	Encourage others to work cooperatively. Keep hands and feet to yourself. It is okay to disagree, but do it without being disagreeable. Be thoughtful of others.	Be thoughtful of others. Keep hands and feet to yourself. Use indoor voices. When moving in room and hallway, always walk on the right side.

Expected Behavior (Middle School)

Expectation	Start of class	Individual work	Teacher lecture	Group work	End of class
Be on time and prepared.	Arrive on time to class. Bring your notebook and writing materials. Listen when Mrs. Jones starts class (only one person speaks at a time).	Be focused on your work and ignore distractions. Remember to follow procedures for all individual assignments. Organize your work and get to work quickly after directed by Mrs. Jones.	Be focused on the current unit of instruction. Use your notebook for taking notes. Please listen and follow along when Mrs. Jones is speaking (only one person speaks at a time).	Be focused on the task to be completed (on task). Have your notebook opened to the proper section being covered. Organize as a team quickly, and start work promptly (within 1 minute).	Adequately prepare materials to leave the classroom (e.g., place only your materials in your binder). Leave the classroom promptly when dismissed by Mrs. Jones.
Be responsible for your actions.	Arrive on time to class. Listen when Mrs. Jones starts class (only one person speaks at a time). Come prepared by completing all assignments and readings.	Remember to follow procedures for individual work. Organize and do the best work that you can, even on a bad day. Control your actions and make your time productive.	Listen and think about points raised in Mrs. Jones' comments. Ask questions of Mrs. Jones and respond to questions. Gain attention by raising your hand; be patient.	Pay attention to your work and only your work. One person speaks at a time. Ask for help as needed. Successfully complete task within allotted time frame.	Be sure you have written down all assignments to be completed prior to next class. Leave classroom in the same condition you found it when you arrived.

(continued)

Expected Behavior (Middle School) *(continued)*

Expectation	Start of class	Individual work	Teacher lecture	Group work	End of class
	Follow all directions provided by Mrs. Jones as you enter the room.			Share roles on the team (e.g., recorder/time keeper).	
Be respectful toward others.	Say "hello" to others using appropriate voice and language before class starts. Listen when Mrs. Jones starts class (only one person speaks at a time). Help others if asked for help.	Get to work quickly on individual work. Be on task and work quietly. Raise hand to get Mrs. Jones' attention.	Please follow along when Mrs. Jones is speaking (only one person speaks at a time). Think about what Mrs. Jones is saying.	Encourage others to be on task. Organize as a team quickly, and start work promptly (within 1 minute). Strive for consensus whenever possible.	Be patient and wait your turn if you need to speak with Mrs. Jones after class. Leave the room in an orderly manner.

Performance Expectations (High School)

Expectation	Start of class	During individual tests	During lecture in class	During other team activities	Outside of class time preparation
Be here/Be ready • On time • Prepared	Arrive on time to class. Bring your notebook and writing materials. Listen when Mr. Smith starts talking (only one person speaks at a time).	Be focused on the current unit tests. Remember to follow procedures for individual tests. Organize and get to work promptly.	Be focused on the current unit of instruction. Use your notebook for taking notes. Please listen and follow along when Mr. Smith is speaking (only one person speaks at a time).	Be focused on the task to be completed (on task). Have your materials open to the proper section being covered. Organize as a team quickly, and start work promptly (within 1 minute).	Review prior class notes before next class. Adequately prepare by doing readings and assignments. Keep your materials organized.
Be responsible • Quality work • Collaborate	Arrive on time to class. Listen when Mr. Smith starts talking (only one person speaks at a time). Come prepared by completing all assignments and readings.	Remember to follow procedures for individual tests. Organize and get to work promptly; make a good effort on each question. Be on task and ask for clarification as needed from Mr. Smith.	Listen and think about points raised in the lecture. Ask questions and respond to questions. Share your perspective on relevant issues to the topic at hand.	Be on task. One person speaks at a time. Ask for help as needed. Successfully complete task within allotted time frame.	Review prior class notes before next class. Adequately prepare by doing readings and assignments. Keep your materials organized.

(continued)

Performance Expectations (High School) *(continued)*

Expectation	Start of class	During individual tests	During lecture in class	During other team activities	Outside of class time preparation
	Follow procedures in course organizer if you miss a class.			Share roles on the team (e.g., recorder/time keeper).	
Be respectful • Encourage others • Recognize others	Politely greet classmates and teacher when arriving to class. Ask others how things are going. Listen when Mr. Smith starts talking (only one person speaks at a time). Provide guidance to classmates who may have been absent from last class.	Get to work quickly on individual tests. Be on task, and work quietly.	Please listen and follow along when Mr. Smith is speaking (only one person speaks at a time). Think about the concepts and practices being described; get the most you can out of the class.	Encourage others to be on task and to provide their perspective. Organize as a team quickly and start work promptly (within 1 minute). Strive for consensus wherever possible.	Review prior class notes before next class. Adequately prepare by doing readings and assignments. Keep your materials organized.

Strategies for Self-Monitoring the 4:1 Ratio in the Classroom

Strategy 1

Group: Place 20 pieces of unpopped popcorn in one pocket and 20 pieces of unpopped popcorn in another pocket at the start of the day. Remove one kernel of corn from your right pocket every time you "catch a kid being good" and provide reinforcement to that same child for following the behavioral expectations. Remove one kernel of corn from your left pocket every time you provide behavioral correction to one of your kids during this same day. At the end of the day, tally up how many kernels you have left in your pockets and then calculate a ratio based on your count (e.g., zero kernels remaining in your right pocket [20 delivered] versus 15 remaining in your left pocket [5 delivered] converts to a 4:1 ratio of positive reinforcement versus corrective feedback). You may also vary the time interval as you see appropriate (e.g., 1 hour versus an entire day).

Individual: Replicate the group process, but focus on a given child as warranted.

Strategy 2

Group: Loosely wrap a piece of masking tape around your right wrist and your left wrist. Have a marker in your pocket. Place one slash mark on the tape around your right wrist for every time you "catch a kid being good" and provide reinforcement to that same child for following the behavioral expectations. Place a slash mark on your left wrist every time you provide behavioral correction to one of your kids during the same day. At the end of the day, tally how many slashes you have on your right wrist and on your left wrist and then calculate a ratio based on your count (e.g., 20 slashes on right wrist versus 5 slashes on left wrist converts to a 4:1 ratio of positive reinforcement versus corrective feedback). You may also vary the time interval as you see appropriate (e.g., 1 hour versus an entire day).

Individual: Replicate the group process, but focus on a given child as warranted.

Behavior Contract

Student name: __Carl__   Today's date: __10/10/07__

Relevant staff name(s):   __John Smith__
                              __Jane Goode__
                              __Carly Smith__
                              __Bob Pevey__
                              __Isham Kalou__

Target behavior (behavioral expectation):
Be respectful: Use appropriate language.
            One person speaks at a time.
            Listen and follow directions the first time.
            Speak only at appropriate times; listen to others when they are speaking.
            Use an indoor voice when speaking.

Data collection procedure:
Use a good behavior chart with "+" for appropriate and "–" for inappropriate behavior.
Teachers and Carl independently evaluate Carl's behavior twice per class period (half
way and at end of each class).

Reinforcement procedure (what and how often):
Carl can choose from a Choice Box (e.g., box containing homework pass, 10 minutes
of extra computer time) at the end of each day when he has earned 7 of 10 "+."

What must student do to earn reinforcement?
Be respectful: Use appropriate language.
            One person speaks at a time.
            Listen and follow directions the first time.
            Speak only at appropriate times; listen to others when they are speaking.
            Use an indoor voice when speaking.
            7 of 10 "+" earned each day

Consequences for failure to meet behavioral expectations:

Carl will not earn access to Choice Box.

Other relevant consequences deemed necessary by teacher(s)

Bonus for exceptional behavioral performance:

When Carl meets expectations 5 consecutive days in a row, he may make a random choice from the Grand Prize Box (e.g., box containing coupons to local sandwich shop, free movie pass, one free video rental). When Carl earns two consecutive bonus picks, we will renegotiate the contract.

Signatures of all relevant people: